CONTENTS

Alex Gordon
Editor

Gerda Gordon
Co-ordinator

Publisher **Ken Laird**
Lang Syne Publishers Ltd.
79 Main Street,
Newtongrange,
Midlothian EH22 4NA
Tel: 0131 344 0414
E Fax: 0845 075 6085
mail: info@lang-syne.co.uk
www.langsyneshop.co.uk

Design **Dorothy Meikle**

Pictures
Vagelis Georgogarion

Print **Printwell Ltd**

Lang**Syne**
PUBLISHING
WRITING *to* REMEMBER

GOAL-DEN BHOYS...matchwinner Odsonne Edouard and his triumphant Celtic team-mates celebrate his second strike in the Scottish Cup Final.

HAPPY BHOYS...Scott Brown and Jonny Hayes lead the parade at the end – and the remarkable treble-treble is accomplished.

SCOTTISH CUP ACTION

THE FLICK OF TIME...Odsonne Edouard lobs the second goal over Hearts keeper Bobby Zlamal as Scott Sinclair looks on.

FRENCH FANCY...Edouard races away in triumph.

HAMPDEN HURRAH...Edouard is about to be congratulated after his dramatic late strike.

PRIZE GUY...Edouard laps up the applause.

SIGN OF THE TIMES...Hampden lights up as Sinclair and James Forrest race to congratulate the goalscorer.

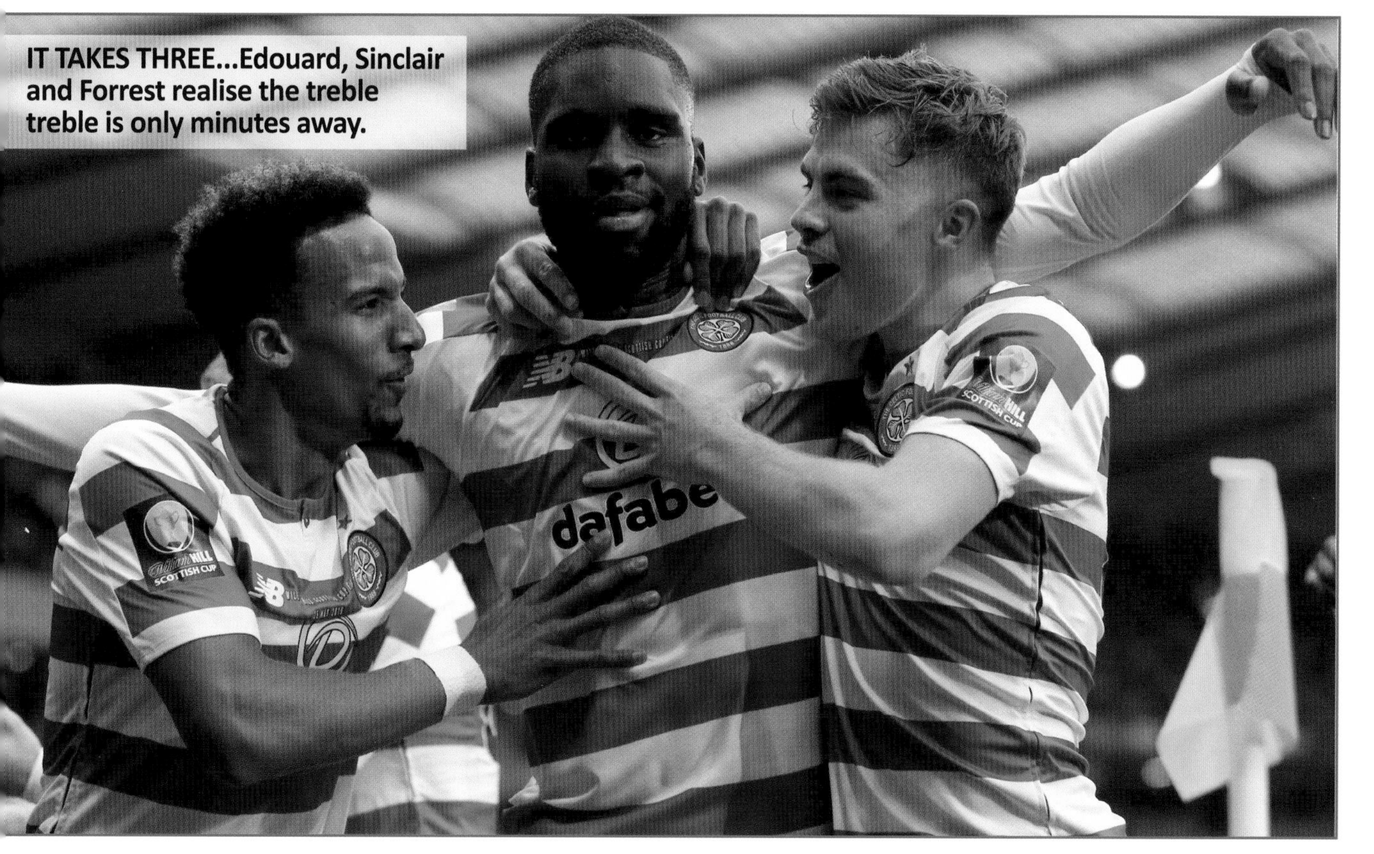

IT TAKES THREE...Edouard, Sinclair and Forrest realise the treble treble is only minutes away.

SCOTTISH CUP ACTION

ON THE SPOT...Bobby Zlamal is booked by referee Willie Collum at the penalty-kick incident.

BURSTING THE HEARTS BALLOON... Edouard at the start of the game.

CHEERS... Edouard and Sinclair share the joy.

NICE AND EASY DOES IT...Edouard slots in the penalty-kick for the Hoops' leveller with Hearts defender Sean Clare getting a close-up view.

THE EQUALISER...Edouard is about to be congratulated by a joyful Callum McGregor.

SCOTTISH CUP ACTION

HIGH AND MIGHTY...Jozo Simunovic clears from Steven MacLean.

CRUNCH... Tom Rogic takes to the air after a challenge from John Souttar.

BEST FOOT FORWARD...Mikey Johnston shows his tricks.

BY THE LEFT...Jonny Hayes takes on Michael Smith.

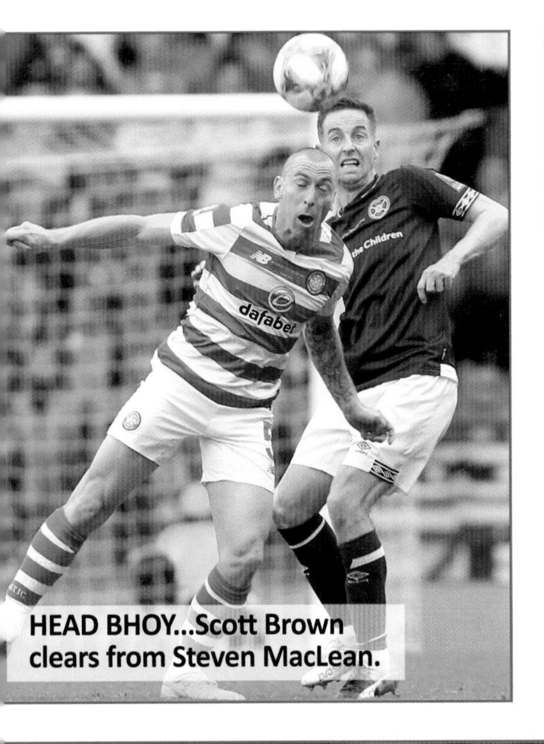

HEAD BHOY...Scott Brown clears from Steven MacLean.

SWEDE DREAMS... Mikael Lustig clears from Ryan Edwards.

AIR WE GO...Sean Clare is flying high after a challenge from Tom Rogic.

SCOTTISH CUP ACTION

GREAT SCOTT...Sinclair with the silverware.

NORWEGIAN GIANT...
Kristoffer Ajer celebrates.

CUP THAT CHEERS...Scott
Brown and his team mates
parade the silverware.

THE GLEE CLUB...delighted Scott Brown gives the thumbs up to the fans at the end.

SCOTTISH CUP ACTION

THREE CHEERS...Scott Brown, Mikael Lustig and Scott Bain with the silverware.

HAMPDEN LIGHT SHOW... the happy Hoops after the Cup presentation.

SEASON 2018/2019

JOY PARADE...Celtic players collect their history-breaking ninth successive domestic trophy.

END GAME... Neil Lennon sinks to his knees.

CONGRATS... Craig Levein and Lennon at final whistle.

CUP OF DREAMS... comeback boss with his reward.

CHAMPAGNE SKIPPER...Scott Brown is sprayed with bubbly.

The Invincibles

No stopping Celts after five-goal romp

UNBEATABLE...skipper Scott Brown and his joyous colleagues celebrate the first title success during Brendan Rodgers' stint.

ALL eyes were riveted on Brendan Rodgers as he led Celtic into their fourth Premiership confrontation of the 2016/17 season following three successive league victories.

Lincoln Red Imps had provided a banana skin in Gibraltar in the Irishman's first competitive game as the manager of his boyhood favourites.

Disaster, of course, was averted in the second leg with three quickfire first-half goals, but it had still been a bit of a jolt to see the best team in Scotland turned over by a bunch of semi-professionals with the local cop scoring the only goal of a Champions League qualifier, irrespective of dodgy playing conditions.

Composure had been sufficiently restored to claim three points in a 2-1 victory against Hearts at Tynecastle followed by a 4-2 triumph over St Johnstone at McDiarmid Park. A week later, the performance was cranked up a notch with a fine, free-flowing 4-1 win over Aberdeen in the east end of Glasgow.

Now, though, there was an exceptionally intriguing confrontation looming on September 10, Rodgers' first meeting with Rangers. It was imperative the new manager made a vibrant first impression with his new followers. Ronny Deila, his predecessor, understood his two-year reign was at an end when Celtic went out of the Scottish Cup at the semi-final stage following a disastrous display against the Ibrox side, who were still in the Championship at the time.

There were murmurs of discontent over the team's lack of progress in Europe under the guidance of the Norwegian, but any stay of execution was obliterated at Hampden on a grey April day after an embarrassing dismissal 5-4 on penalty-kicks following extra-time and a 2-2 stalemate. There was no safety net for Deila and the appointment of Rodgers was hastened after events that day in the south side of Glasgow.

And so the former Liverpool manager took his place in the dug-out on a sun-kissed afternoon at his new home. He was not to know that his four Old Firm matches in his debut term as the club's inspirational team boss was to start and end with 5-1 triumphs. And, after the hiccup in the

SEASON 2016/2017

Scottish Premier League Table

P	Team	Pld	W	D	L	GF	GA	GD	Pts
1	**Celtic**	**38**	**34**	**4**	**0**	**106**	**25**	**+81**	**106**
2	Aberdeen	38	24	4	10	74	35	+39	76
3	Rangers	38	19	10	9	56	44	+12	67
4	St Johnstone	38	17	7	14	50	46	+4	58
5	Heart of Midlothian	38	12	10	16	55	52	+3	46
6	Partick Thistle	38	10	12	16	38	54	−16	42
7	Ross County	38	11	13	14	48	58	−10	46
8	Kilmarnock	38	9	14	15	36	56	−20	41
9	Motherwell	38	10	8	20	46	69	−23	38
10	Dundee	38	10	7	21	38	62	−24	37
11	Hamilton Academical	38	7	14	17	37	56	−19	35
12	Inverness Caledonian Thistle	38	7	13	18	44	71	−27	34

League Cup Final

November 27, 2017:
CELTIC 3 Rogic, Forrest, Dembele (pen)
ABERDEEN 0

Gordon; Lustig, Simunovic, Sviatchneko, Izaguirre; Brown, Rogic (sub: McGregor); Roberts (sub: Bitton), Armstrong, Forrest (sub: Griffiths); Dembele.

Scottish Cup Final

May 27, 2017: **CELTIC 2** Armstrong, Rogic
ABERDEEN 1 Hayes

Gordon; Lustig, Simunovic, Boyata, Tierney (sub: Rogic); Brown, Armstrong; Roberts (sub: Sviatchenko), McGregor, Sinclair; Griffiths.

WELCOME...Brendan Rodgers makes his first appearance as Celtic manager at Parkhead in May 2016.

PREMIERSHIP

CRASH LANDING...Leigh Griffiths is floored after a challenge from St. Johnstone defender Richard Foster.

FIVE AGAINST ONE...Jozo Simunovic puts the pressure on the Motherwell defence.

FLASH GORDON...Celtic keeper Craig Gordon makes a brilliant save against Aberdeen.

AERIAL ANTICS...Moussa Dembele tries an acrobatic effort against Dundee.

DOWN BUT NOT OUT... Scott Sinclair is grounded on this occasion, but he finished his debut season with twenty-five goals.

shadow of the Rock of Gibraltar, the team were to go through an entire domestic season without loss to earn the tag The Invincibles.

Rodgers got the ball rolling in Paradise and saw it through until the trip across the River Clyde seven months later. In between on points-gathering business, there had been a 2-1 success on Hogmanay at Ibrox and a 1-1 draw at home where victory was an elusive three minutes away. It had been an incredible and breathtaking journey for the manager.

There were also the little matters of a 1-0 success in the League Cup semi-final over the team bossed by Mark Warburton and then the 2-0 Scottish Cup last-four victory over the side now managed by Portuguese coach Pedro Caixinha.

One small blip in the radar of six Glasgow derbies was allowed, apparently.

A Hollywood scriptwriter with the most vivid imagination couldn't have done a better job for Rodgers. In the opening tussle, Moussa Dembele, only twenty years old and bought from Fulham for a bargain £500,000 in the summer, went on the rampage. The muscular French youngster was brought in to replaced the injured Leigh Griffiths and simply ran amok with a perfect hat-trick – one with his head, one with his right foot and one with his left – as he shredded a bewildered opposing defence. The 60,000 crowd watched transfixed as he put Rangers to the sword.

Remarkably, it took Celtic until the thirty-fourth minute to claim the breakthrough goal. Scott Sinclair swung over a left-wing corner-kick and the juggernaut frontman was unmarked as he sent a header thudding into the net. Eight minutes later, Dembele doubled his team's advantage when he latched onto a threaded pass from Nir Bitton, then sauntered away from the flummoxed Phillipe Senderos before leaving exposed keeper Wes Foderingham helpless with a neat right-foot finish.

Just before the interval, Dorus de Vries, the keeper bought from Nottingham Forest to team up again with his former Swansea manager Rodgers, elected to remain on his line as James Tavernier swung over a right-wing cross. Kenny Miller met it at the back post to loop a header over the Dutch goalie and Joe Garner bundled the ball over the line from practically under the crossbar. The half-time scoreline hardly reflected the home side's overall superiority.

In the sixty-first minute, Rodgers smiled as he witnessed his side extend their advantage again when Man of the Match Dembele released a pass to Scott Sinclair who finished with anticipated accuracy. In the eighty-first minute Rangers' new signing Senderos, who just couldn't cope with the energetic Gallic giant, was sent off following a second yellow card for a senseless handball. The former Swiss international looked almost relieved to be exiting the painful proceedings. Two minutes later, Dembele completed his terrific threesome when Mikael Lustig sent over a neat cross from the right and the frontman killed it in one movement before lashing a left-foot drive into the corner of the net.

Stuart Armstrong, who had replaced Tom Rogic in the fifty-fourth minute, made the most of some slick lead-up play between Sinclair and Kieran Tierney to thump a low drive beyond the overworked Foderingham for the fifth and final goal as the champions finished with a flourish. It had been a day to remember for a young Frenchman and a forty-four-year-old Irishman.

Rodgers was purring with satisfaction again as 2016 ebbed into a New Year. Celtic had already played eight games in December as they prepared for the Hogmanay confrontation at Ibrox. With praiseworthy consistency, the Irishman's side had won seven of those outings with the other drawn, a 1-1 Champions League stalemate against Manchester City at The Etihad.

Motherwell, Partick Thistle (twice), Hamilton Accies (twice), Dundee and Ross County had been met and vanquished en route to the second Premiership meeting of the season against Warburton's team in Govan before bringing down the curtain on an eventful 2016 for all concerned with the Parkhead club.

Celtic knew a win would see them go nineteen points ahead of their Glasgow neighbours, a victory that would most assuredly leave them in their slipstream for the rest of the league season. However, the task became a bit more onerous when Rangers took the lead in the twelfth minute. Danish defender Erik Sviatchenko played an unwitting and unexpected role with a sloppy pass straight to Kenny Miller. He knocked it wide to James Tavernier, who played a quick one-two with Josh Windass to get round the back of the defence before zipping a right-wing cross into the penalty area. Miller, racing in at speed, turned the ball home from three yards.

In the thirty-third minute, there was relief all round among the travelling support when Rodgers' side equalised. Moments earlier, Scott Sinclair had left Wes Foderingham helpless with a sweeping low effort that smacked against the inside of the left-hand upright before Clint Hill hastily booted the rebound for a corner-kick. Sinclair stepped up to take the award and Moussa Dembele, scorer of three goals in the previous league meeting of the teams, eluded his marker Danny Wilson at the far post. He took a touch with his right foot and then lashed in an unstoppable left-foot howitzer that thundered into the roof of the net.

TAKE THAT...Scott Sinclair scores the winner in the Hogmanay clash at Ibrox.

Ten minutes after the turnaround, the French striking sensation almost repeated the feat when he met a deft left-wing cross from Callum McGregor in acrobatic fashion, but the ball bounced up off the turf past a bamboozled Foderingham and clattered against the face of the crossbar and the chance was lost.

Celtic were not to be denied, though. In the sixty-eighth minute, Rodgers took off James Forrest and introduced substitute Patrick Roberts. It turned out to be a shrewd move from the manager. Within two minutes, the tricky, little winger helped set up the winner. He threaded an exquisite pass through the home rearguard into the path of Stuart Armstrong on the right. He swiftly squared it across the face of the goal and Sinclair had read his intentions perfectly. He was left in splendid isolation to roll the ball into the net at the back post.

"It was a brilliant result and a really glad advert for Scottish football. Both sets of players, did very well considering the conditions. but I thought we thoroughly deserved to win," said Rodgers.

He wasn't quite so satisfied, however, after the third confrontation with the team's city foes who had parted way with boss Mark Warburton and replaced him with caretaker Graeme Murty who had stepped up from coaching the Under-20s.

On the afternoon of March 12 in the east end of Glasgow, the clock was ticking down as Celtic protected Stuart Armstrong's thirty-fifth minute effort. They looked comfortable enough, but calamity struck in the eighty-seventh minute when some unusually lackadaisical defending allowed an opening for the Ibrox men. Emerson Hyndman was allowed a clear shot at goal from just inside the box and the on-loan Bournemouth midfielder fired in a ferocious low drive.

Craig Gordon spread his 6ft 4in frame as he dived to his right to push the ball away. Alas, it went straight to veteran centre-half Clint Hill, lurking at the far post. Before Mikael Lustig could react, the defender, with reflexes belying his thirty-eight years, sped in to snap up the opportunity from practically on the goal-line to ram the equaliser into the net.

Apart from a pocket of visiting fans, Celtic Park fell silent; no-one saw that one coming. It looked as though another three points were about to be claimed after the first-half opener from Armstrong, who had earlier struck the post with a clever free-kick. However, shortly afterwards he worked a swift manoeuvre with James Forrest and walloped a left-foot drive from sixteen yards low past Wes Foderingham.

The encounter ended on a controversial note when referee Bobby Madden refused what looked to many like an indisputable penalty-kick in the fading seconds. Hill, who had previously been booked, clearly attempted to pull back Leigh Griffiths outside the box before the elusive striker raced clear. The defender then lunged in to send the Celtic player crashing to the ground. Penalty-kick? It certainly would have been given by most match officials, but, astoundingly, Madden waved away the claims.

In the end, Celtic had to be content with a draw that kept them thirty-three points ahead of the Ibrox side. They also knew they would lift their sixth successive Premiership crown if they won their next two games against Dundee and Hearts.

THE WINNER... Stuart Armstrong hits the clincher against Kilmarnock.

BAWL BHOY... Scott Brown urges on his troops.

CHARGE...Moussa Dembele takes on Aberdeen defender Anthony O'Connor.

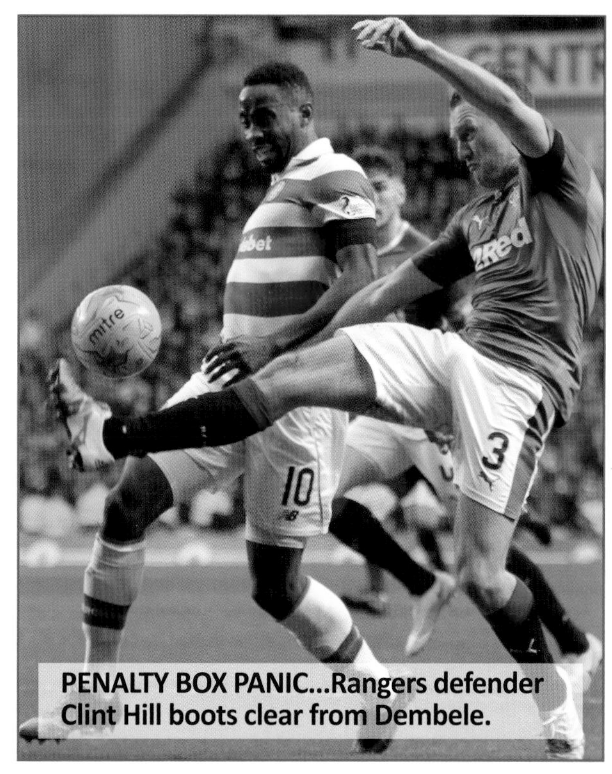

PENALTY BOX PANIC...Rangers defender Clint Hill boots clear from Dembele.

WELL HELD...Craig Gordon catches a cross at Tynecastle.

NETBOUND...Scott Sinclair slams a shot past Hearts keeper Jack Hamilton.

PREMIERSHIP

DREAM BHOY...Kieran Tierney with the Premiership trophy.

TAKE THAT...Scott Sinclair is about to be congratulated by Tom Rogic after another goal.

BIG HAND...Callum McGregor, Leigh Griffiths, Kieran Tierney and Mikael Lustig celebrate.

PARADISE...Brendan Rodgers after his first title success.

IN THE BLACK...James Forrest and Leigh Griffiths show their delight.

THREE'S A PARTY...James Forrest, Leigh Griffiths and Scott Brown display their delight.

Rodgers said: "We obviously should have had a penalty-
.ck right at the death. It was a clear-cut penalty. It's very
ustrating, especially when Clint Hill tells me he got away
ith it on the pitch, so that's even more so. Clint's a good
ıy, an honest fella and I know when he says it, he knows
e got away with one. Probably everyone has seen it apart
om the referee.

"It's always disappointing if you lose an equaliser late on
ke that, especially the manner of it. But that's the way it
)es sometimes. I'm proud of the team, although I don't
ink we were so good in the first-half. However, I thought
e commitment was great and, in the second-half, I thought
was maybe a matter of time before we got our second goal,
ut when it's at 1-0 there is always that little moment that
ın happen."

There was no such anxiety for Rodgers at Ibrox in the
ext clash on April 29. On this occasion, there were to be
o lifelines for the home team or their latest managerial
ppointment, Pedro Caixinha. Extraordinarily, Rodgers, in
is first season at Celtic, had faced three different opponents
ı the Rangers dug-out.

The Portuguese gaffer looked on in bewilderment and
orror as his side were swept away by a green-and-white
hirlwind as Celtic hammered in five goals at Ibrox for the
rst time in their history.

The visitors took the lead in the seventh minute and were
elentless as they hunted down their foes in pursuit of even
ore glory. A last-ditch tackle from Clint Hill prevented
allum McGregor from opening the scoring in sixty-five
econds, but he only delayed the inevitable agony. Teenage
ft-back Myles Beerman was reckless with a sliding
hallenge on speeding Patrick Roberts and he sent the winger sprawling in the penalty box. Referee John Beaton pointed to the spot and Scott Sinclair sent the ball spinning into the corner of the net with Wes Foderingham taking off in the opposite direction.

In the eighteenth minute, the keeper revisited the back of his rigging to fetch the ball for a second time. Stuart Armstrong released a pass to Leigh Griffiths on the left. He took a touch and, from an angle, unleashed a pulverising left-foot drive that zoomed over the goalie's hands into the net. The procession towards the Rangers goal continued unabated for the remaining twenty-seven minutes of the half. Griffiths hit the crossbar and Sinclair put the rebound wide of the empty net. The Englishman then missed from two yards after a neat lob over from the left by Griffiths.

The second-half was only seven minutes old when the champions struck again. The busy and clever Roberts retrieved a misplaced pass to poke the ball in front of McGregor, who resisted the temptation to hit a first-time shot. He nurtured the ball, waited for a moment and then placed a cunning shot through the legs of James Tavernier and wide of the sprawling Foderingham. In the sixty-sixth minute, the flustered Beerman clattered Roberts once again and Griffiths delicately swung over the resultant free-kick. The keeper was rooted to his line and Dedryck Boyata took full advantage as he rose to nod the ball down and into the net.

There was a moment's respite for the well-trounced home side in the eighty-first minute when Kenny Miller worked a quick one-two with Joe Garner and placed an effort wide of Craig Gordon. Celtic kept the best to the last. Three minutes remained when Mikael Lustig picked up a loose ball and careered towards the danger zone. Displaying mesmerising ▶

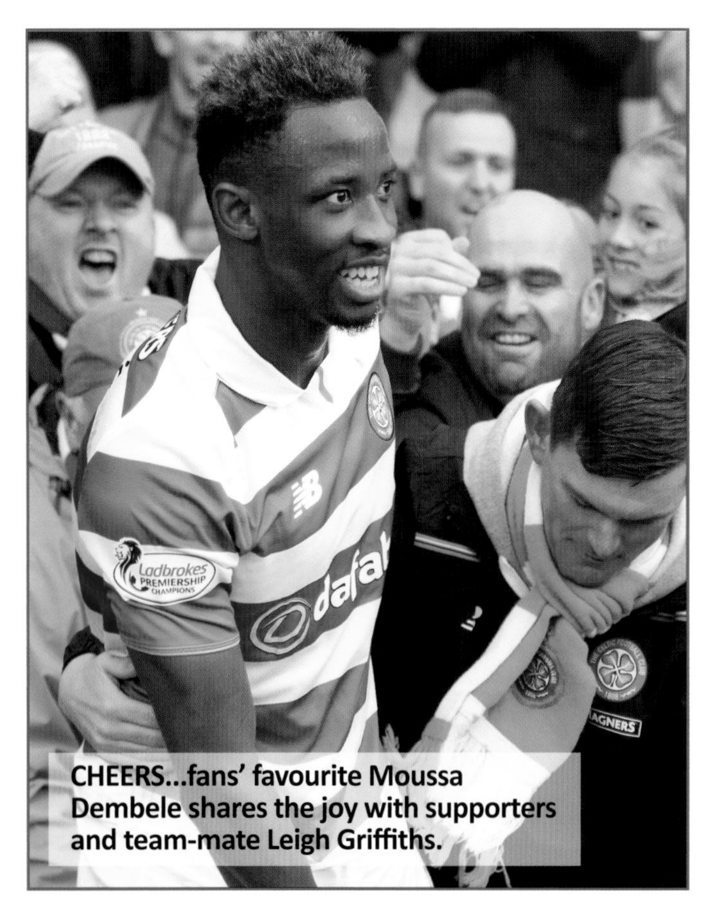

CHEERS...fans' favourite Moussa Dembele shares the joy with supporters and team-mate Leigh Griffiths.

skills, the Swedish international defender manoeuvred his way past Danny Wilson, lined up a shot from the edge of the box and gracefully caressed the ball towards its destination.

Rodgers said: "It was an outstanding team performance. From the very first whistle, we were exceptional. The only disappointment was we could have scored more goals. We created really good chances to get more. Fundamentally, the players pressed the game very well. Our tactical organisation for getting the ball back was the key.

"A lot of our game has improved as the season has gone on. I said when I came in, we would get better and better. If you compare this 5-1 to the 5-1 earlier this season, there's a big difference for me in terms of tactical organisation and players understanding concepts of what we are trying to do. Collectively, they all understand their roles in getting forward, who needs to score goals and who needs to be effective."

Back on August 7 the previous year in Edinburgh, there were signs that this Celtic team, with Rodgers the new man with his hand on the tiller, were a different breed from the one witnessed under Ronny Deila who found great difficulties in the step up from Norwegian football where he had earned the reputation as a good coach with sound philosophies. The intensity of managing at a team of Celtic's magnitude saw him struggle although, to be fair, he still managed to keep the title run going with back-to-back successes during his stay.

Rodgers had tracked his former Swansea attacker Scott Sinclair for about a month before he finally got his man as relegated Aston Villa accepted a fee that would rise to £4.5million with add-ons. Money well spent, declared the champions' followers in the near-17,000 Tynecastle crowd after witnessing the Englishman in action against Hearts fo under half-an-hour.

His transfer had only been agreed the previous afternoo and Celtic rushed through his registration to make sure he was eligible to play. Rodgers left him on the substitutes' bench at the start, but he replaced Stuart Armstrong in the sixty-first minute with the score stalemated at 1-1.

Rodgers applauded his side's first goal in the Premiershi in the eighth minute when Callum McGregor was sent spinning under a challenge and the ball swept to James Forrest. Without breaking stride, the winger struck the ball with the outside of his right foot and his screamer left Jack Hamilton helpless low to his right.

Referee John Beaton wrongly awarded the Edinburgh side a penalty-kick leveller in the thirty-sixth minute after Jamie Walker had taken an obvious dive when Kieran Tierney checked out of a tackle. The whistler was conned and the player was later banned for simulation. That was of little consequence to Celtic, however, when Walker drilled the award beyond Craig Gordon.

The game looked to be heading for a draw until the entrance from Sinclair and his immediate impact. Running more than half the length of the field as Rodgers' men hit on the break, the new Bhoy arrived smack on time to hammer a sublime left-wing delivery from Leigh Griffiths into the ne for the winner.

Celtic – and Sinclair who completed the campaign with twenty-five goals – had started as they clearly meant to continue and finish.

The Rodgers Regime was up and running. Good times la ahead. ■

GOVAN GLEE...Sinclair celebrates Ibrox winner with sub Leigh Griffiths.

EMOTIONAL GUY...Leigh Griffiths in the thick of the action against Dundee.

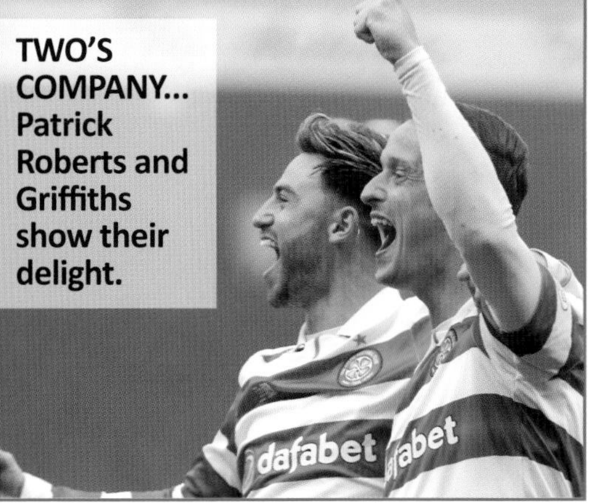

TWO'S COMPANY... Patrick Roberts and Griffiths show their delight.

STRAIGHT FROM THE HEART...Tom Rogic after scoring at Aberdeen.

ONE-SEASON WONDER...Kolo Toure had a year at the champions.

CAPITAL GAINS...Scott Sinclair is congratulated by Kieran Tierney after a goal at Tynecastle.

WHO LOVES YOU... Stuart Armstrong blows kisses to the crowd.

PREMIERSHIP

Premiership Results

August 7, 2016: **HEARTS 1** Walker (pen)
CELTIC 2 Forrest, Sinclair
Gordon; Lustig, Toure, O'Connell (sub: Rogic), Tierney; Forrest, Brown, Armstrong (sub: Sinclair), McGregor; Dembele, Griffiths (sub: Janko).

August 20: **ST JOHNSTONE 2** Swanson (pen), MacLean
CELTIC 4 Griffiths, Sinclair, Forrest, Christie
Gordon; Janko, Toure, O'Connell, Tierney; Brown, Bitton (sub: Henderson); Forrest (sub: Christie), Rogic, Sinclair; Griffiths (sub: Dembele).

August 27: **CELTIC 4** Griffiths, Forrest, Sinclair (pen), Rogic
ABERDEEN 1 Rooney
De Vries; Lustig, Toure, Sviatchenko, Tierney; Brown, Bitton (sub: McGregor); Forrest, Rogic, Sinclair; Griffiths (Dembele).

September 10: **CELTIC 5** Dembele (3), Sinclair, Armstrong
RANGERS 1 Garner
De Vries; Lustig, Toure, Sviatchenko, Tierney; Brown (sub: McGregor), Bitton; Forrest (sub: Roberts), Rogic (sub: Armstrong), Sinclair; Dembele.

September 18: **INVERNESS CALEY THISTLE 2** King, Fisher
CELTIC 2 Rogic, Sinclair
De Vries; Gamboa (sub: Simunovic), Lustig, Sviatchenko, Tierney; Brown, Rogic (sub: Armstrong); Roberts (sub: Forrest), McGregor, Sinclair; Dembele.

September 24: **CELTIC 6** Dembele (2), Forrest, Griffiths, Sinclair (pen), Rogic
KILMARNOCK 1 Coulibaly
De Vries (sub: Gordon); Lustig, Simunovic, Sviatchenko, Tierney; Brown, Bitton; Forrest, Rogic, Sinclair (sub: Roberts); Dembele (sub: Griffiths).

October 1: **DUNDEE 0**
CELTIC 1 Brown
Gordon; Lustig, Simunovic, Sviatchenko, Tierney; Brown, Bitton; Forrest (sub: Roberts), Rogic (sub: Griffiths), Sinclair (sub: Armstrong); Dembele.

October 15: **CELTIC 2** Sinclair, Dembele (pen)
MOTHERWELL 0
Gordon; Gamboa (sub: Griffiths), Simunovic, Sviatchenko, Tierney; Brown, Henderson; Forrest (sub: Toure), Armstrong (sub: Roberts), Sinclair; Dembele.

October 26: **ROSS COUNTY 0**
CELTIC 4 Roberts, Armstrong, Sinclair, Dembele
Gordon; Gamboa, Lustig, Sviatchenko, Izaguirre; McGregor, Henderson (sub: Sinclair); Roberts, Armstrong, Christie (sub: Dembele); Griffiths (sub: Bitton).

October 29: **ABERDEEN 0**
CELTIC 1 Rogic
Gordon; Lustig (sub: Gamboa), Simunovic, Sviatchenko, Izaguirre; Brown, Rogic (sub: Bitton); Forrest (sub: Roberts), Armstrong, Sinclair; Dembele.

November 5: **CELTIC 3** Sinclair, Griffiths, Rogic
INVERNESS CALEY THISTLE 0
Gordon; Lustig (sub: Izaguirre), Simunovic, Sviatchenko; Roberts, Brown (sub: Bitton), Armstrong, McGregor, Sinclair; Dembele (sub: Rogic), Griffiths.

November 18: **KILMARNOCK 0**
CELTIC 1 Armstrong
Gordon; Lustig, Boyata, Sviatchenko, McGregor; Brown, Armstrong; Roberts (sub: Rogic), Sinclair, Forrest (sub: Bitton); Dembele.

December 3: **MOTHERWELL 3** Moult (2), Ainsworth
CELTIC 4 McGregor, Roberts, Armstrong, Rog
Gordon; Lustig, Simunovic, Tiure, Izaguirre (sub: McGregor); Brown, Armstrong; Roberts (sub: Bitton), Rogic, Forrest (sub: Gamboa); Dembele.

December 9: **PARTICK THISTLE 1** Lindsay
CELTIC 4 Armstrong (2), Griffiths, McGregor
Gordon; Gamboa, Lustig, Sviatchenko, Izaguirre; Brown, Armstrong; Roberts (sub: Dembele), Rogic (sub: McGregor), Mackay-Streven (sub: Christie); Griffiths.

December 13: **CELTIC 1** Griffiths
HAMILTON ACCIES 0
Gordon; Lustig, Simunovic, Sviatchenko; Brown, Armstrong; Roberts, Rogic, McGregor (sub: Mackay-Steven); Griffiths, Dembele (sub: Bitton).

December 17: **CELTIC 2** Griffiths, Bitton
DUNDEE 1 Haber
Gordon; Gamboa, Simunovic, Sviatchenko, Izaguirre; Bitton, Armstrong; Christie, Rogic (sub: McGregor), Mackay-Steven (sub: Sinclair); Griffiths (sub: Dembele).

December 20: **CELTIC 1** Sinclair
PARTICK THISTLE 0
Gordon; Gamboa, Lustig, Simunovic, Miller (sub: Izaguirre); Brown, Henderson; Roberts, McGregor, Sinclair (sub: Armstrong); Dembele (sub: Griffiths).

December 24: **HAMILTON ACCIES 0**
CELTIC 3 Griffiths, Armstrong, Dembele
Gordon; Gamboa, Lustig, Sviatchenko, Izaguirre; Brown, Armstrong; Roberts (sub: Bitton), McGregor, Sinclair (sub: Forrest); Griffiths (sub: Dembele).

December 28: **CELTIC 2** Sviatchenko, Armstrong
ROSS COUNTY 0
Gordon; Lustig, Simunovic, Sviatchenko, Izaguirre; Brown, Armstron
Forrest (sub: Roberts), Christie (sub: Henderson), Sinclair; Griffiths (sub: Dembele).

December 31: **RANGERS 1** Miller
CELTIC 2 Dembele, Sinclair
Gordon; Lustig, Simunovic, Sviatchenko, Izaguirre; Brown, Armstron
Forrest (sub: Roberts), McGregor, Sinclair; Dembele.

nuary 25, 2017:
CELTIC 1 Boyata
ST JOHNSTONE 0
ordon; Gamboa (sub: Sviatchenko), Boyata, Simunovic, Tierney; own, Bitton; Forrest (sub: Roberts), Armstrong, Sinclair; Dembele ub: Griffiths).

nuary 29: **CELTIC 4** McGregor, Sinclair (2, 1 pen), Roberts
HEARTS 0
ordon; Gamboa (sub: Lustig), Boyata, Simunovic, Tierney; Brown, tton; Roberts (sub: Aitchison), McGregor, Forrest (sub: Henderson); nclair.

ebruary 1: **CELTIC 1** Boyata
ABERDEEN 0
ordon; Lustig, Boyata, Simunovic, Tierney; Brown, Bitton; oberts (sub: Sviatchenko), McGregor (sub: Henderson), Forrest ub: Mackay-Steven); Sinclair.

ebruary 5: **ST JOHNSTONE 2** Watson, Boyata (og)
CELTIC 5 Henderson, Dembele (3, 1 pen), Sinclair
ordon; Lustig, Boyata, Sviatchenko, Tierney; Brown, Bitton; oberts (sub: Ciftci), Henderson (sub: McGregor), Mackay-Steven ub: Dembele); Sinclair.

ebruary 18: **CELTIC 2** Dembele (pen), Forrest
MOTHERWELL 0
ordon; Lustig, Boyata, Simunovic, Tierney; Brown, Bitton ub: McGregor); Forrest, Henderson (sub: Armstrong), Sinclair; embele.

ebruary 25: **CELTIC 2** Dembele (2, 1 pen)
HAMILTON ACCIES 0
ordon; Gamboa, Boyata, Sviatchenko, Tierney; Brown, Bitton; orrest (sub: Mackay-Steven), Armstrong (sub: McGregor), Sinclair; embele (sub: Griffiths).

larch 1: **INVERNESS CALEY THISTLE 0**
CELTIC 4 Sinclair, Dembele (2), Armstrong
ordon; Lustig, Boyata, Sviatchenko, Tierney; Brown ub: Henderson), Bitton; Mackay-Steven (sub: McGregor), rmstrong, Sinclair; Dembele.

larch 12: **CELTIC 1** Armstrong
RANGERS 1 Hill
ordon; Lustig, Boyata, Sviatchenko, Tierney; Brown, Bitton ub: McGregor); Forrest (sub: Roberts), Armstrong (sub: Griffiths), inclair; Dembele.

larch 19: **DUNDEE 1** El Bakhtaoui
CELTIC 2 Simunovic, Armstrong
ordon; Lustig, Boyata, Simunovic, Tierney; Brown, McGregor ub: Kouassi); Forrest (sub: Roberts), Armstrong, Sinclair ub: Sviatchenko); Dembele.

April 2: **HEARTS 0**
CELTIC 5 Sinclair (3, 1 pen), Armstrong, Roberts
Gordon; Lustig (sub: Gamboa), Boyata (sub: Toure), Simunovic, Tierney; Brown, Armstrong; Forrest, McGregor, Sinclair; Roberts (sub: Mackay-Steven).

April 5: **CELTIC 1** Sinclair
PARTICK THISTLE 1 Azeez
Gordon; Lustig, Simunovic, Sviatchenko; Gamboa, Kouassi (sub: Armstrong), Bitton, Izaguirre (sub: Rogic); Roberts, McGregor (sub: Aitchison), Sinclair.

April 8: **CELTIC 3** Armstrong, Sinclair, Forrest
KILMARNOCK 1 Jones
Gordon; Lustig, Simunovic, Boyata, Tierney; Brown, Armstrong (sub: Kouassi); Forrest, McGregor (sub: Rogic), Sinclair; Roberts (sub: Dembele).

April 16: **ROSS COUNTY 2** Gardyne, Boyce (pen)
CELTIC 2 Tierney, Roberts
Gordon; Simunovic, Sviatchenko, Tierney; Brown, Armstrong; Forrest (sub: Roberts), McGregor, Rogic (sub: Gamboa), Sinclair; Dembele (sub: Griffiths).

April 29: **RANGERS 1** Miller
CELTIC 5 Sinclair (pen), Griffiths, McGregor, Boyata, Lustig
Gordon; Lustig, Simunovic, Boyata, Tierney; Brown (sub: Kouassi), Armstrong (sub: Rogic); Roberts (sub: Forrest), McGregor, Sinclair; Griffiths.

May 6: **CELTIC 4** Roberts (2), Boyata, McGregor
ST JOHNSTONE 1 MacLean
Gordon; Ralston, Simunovic, Boyata, Tierney; Bitton, Armstrong; Roberts (sub: Forrest), Rogic (sub: McGregor), Johnston (sub: Sinclair); Griffiths.

May 12: **ABERDEEN 1** Hayes
CELTIC 3 Boyata, Armstrong, Griffiths
Gordon; Lustig (sub: Sviatchenko), Simunovic, Boyata, Tierney; Rogic (sub: Bitton), Armstrong; Roberts, McGregor, Sinclair; Griffiths (sub: Forrest).

May 18: **PARTICK THISTLE 0**
CELTIC 5 Griffiths (pen), Rogic, Roberts (2), McGregor
Gordon; Gamboa, Sviatchenko, Boyata (sub: Toure), Izaguirre; Brown, McGregor; Roberts, Rogic, Forrest (sub: Bitton); Griffiths (sub: Sinclair).

May 21: **CELTIC 2** Griffiths, Armstrong
HEARTS 0
Gordon; Gamboa (sub: Rogic), Simunovic (sub: Toure), Boyata, Tierney; Brown, Armstrong (sub: Sviatchenko); Roberts, McGregor, Sinclair; Griffiths.

The Ton-Up Bhoys

CELTIC 3 ABERDEEN 0 (November 27, 2016)

Celtic have Final say as they hit the Century

CELTIC went into the League Cup Final of season 2016/17 with the mesmerising opportunity of claiming the club's one hundredth trophy. On a chilly, grey afternoon in November 2016 at Hampden they were ninety minutes away from being crowned Celtic Centurians.

Opponents Aberdeen were determined to make certain there would be no celebrating on the south side of Glasgow that day as they arrived in the city on a raft of promises and positivity. Derek McInnes and his Pittodrie protagonists had made it plain on the days counting down to the confrontation they were not at the national stadium merely to make up the numbers.

Quite the reverse, in fact. The Dons were optimistic of ruining Brendan Rodgers' chance of making history while leading his players to a landmark piece of silverware.

The persuasive noises coming out of the north east of the country had many onlookers convinced there could be a comeuppance for Celtic on such a momentous occasion.

That was until the sixteenth minute when Tom Rogic struck to put Rodgers' men ahead with a sublime goal. That was the moment the talking had to stop.

The classy Australian midfielder, a playmaker who performs with a spring in his step, interrupted proceedings as he elegantly took centre stage. With instant control, he accepted a pass on the right side and gracefully stepped inside Dons skipper Graeme Shinnie onto his educated left foot. He paused for a split-second to size up the situation before swishing a curling effort wide of the groping fingers of the desperately-diving Joe Lewis. The elongated keeper failed to get a touch and the ball nestled behind him as the Celtic fans in the stadium erupted in joy.

Aberdeen had been undone with one exquisite piece of individual artistry. And they could not say they hadn't been warned. Rogic had already put his opponents twice to the sword in previous games in the campaign. He scored in the champions' 4-1 triumph at Parkhead in August and followed ▶

RISE AND SHINE...Mikael Lustig is carried away as he celebrates Tom Rogic's goal against Aberdeen.

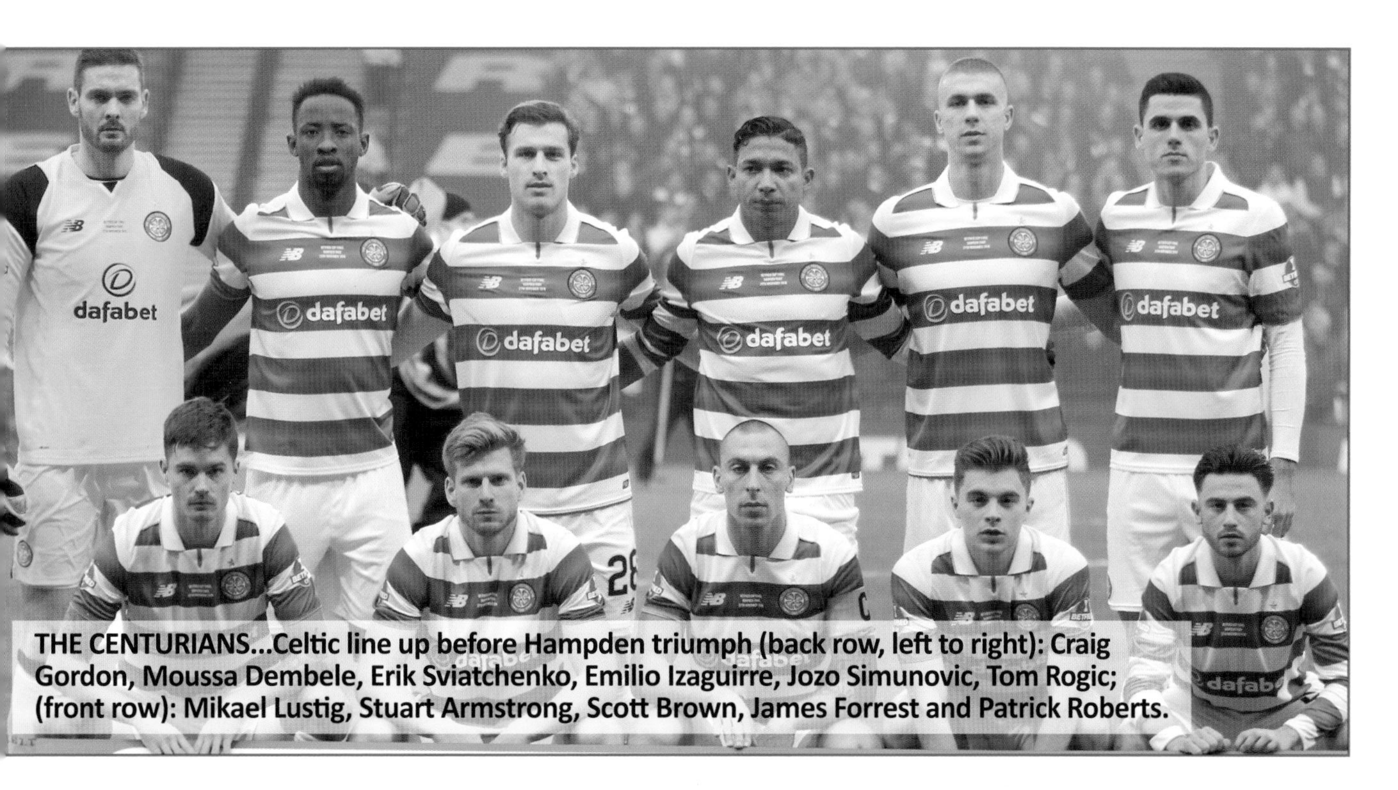
THE CENTURIANS...Celtic line up before Hampden triumph (back row, left to right): Craig Gordon, Moussa Dembele, Erik Sviatchenko, Emilio Izaguirre, Jozo Simunovic, Tom Rogic; (front row): Mikael Lustig, Stuart Armstrong, Scott Brown, James Forrest and Patrick Roberts.

AGONY AND ECSTASY... James Forrest leaves three Dons players grounded after his wonder goal.

SPOT ON...Dembele nets his penalty against the Dons.

HAPPY DAZE...Dembele celebrates with Tom Rogic.

LEAGUE CUP CAMPAIGN

CUP FINAL HERE WE COME...Jozo Simunovic and Erik Sviatchenko clear from Rangers striker Kenny Miller.

THE BHOY DANE GOOD... Sviatchenko heads away from Josh Windass.

THE WINNER... Moussa Dembele nets the only goal.

IN THE NET... Kieran Tierney celebrates.

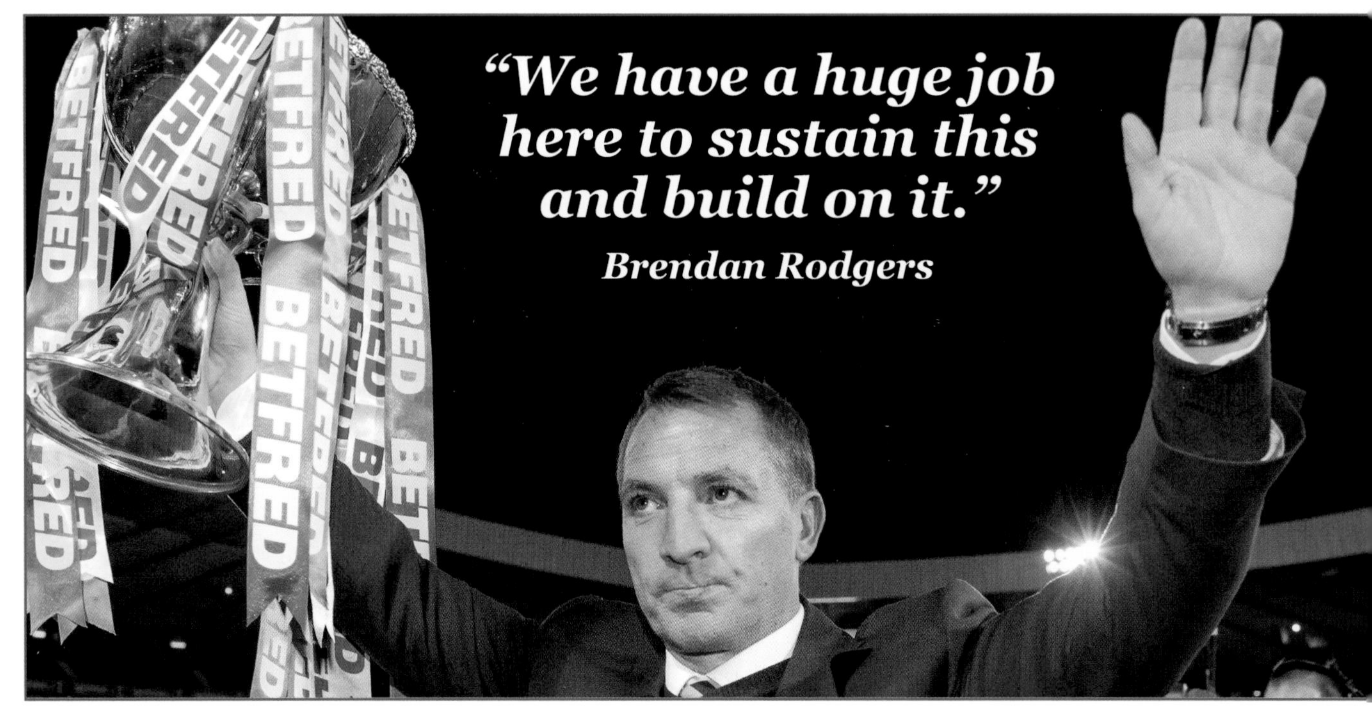

"We have a huge job here to sustain this and build on it."

Brendan Rodgers

hat up with the only goal of a dramatic Pittodrie occasion in)ctober.

Precisely, twenty-four minutes after his team-mate's lassic counter at the national stadium, James Forrest ıtched onto a Rogic pass just inside his own half and odged and swivelled at speed in an extraordinary erpentine-weaving run straight towards the heart of the)ons rearguard. The nimble winger, rejuvenated under the uidance of Brendan Rodgers, drove with menace towards he frantic Lewis.

Defender Andy Considine attempted a last-ditch tackle, ut his timing was out as Forrest took aim and let fly from ust inside the box. His aim was good and true as the ball urtled beyond Lewis at his right-hand side. The ball estled behind the keeper and a section of the attendance ealised their lengthy journey had been in vain; there would e no sensation; the silverware would not be leaving Ǝlasgow.

It was all over in the sixty-fourth minute when Forrest, roducing a Man of the Match performance, latched onto pass from the ever-astute Rogic before being clattered by nthony O'Connor. Penalty-kick, no doubt about it. And ikewise the outcome as Moussa Dembele strode forward urposely and deftly piloted the ball into one corner as Lewis noved to the other.

Scotland international No.1 Craig Gordon, a month efore his thirty-fourth birthday, went through the ournament without conceding a goal and afterwards smiled: That's always important for a keeper and the men in front f him. And we've got guys who can score goals from all ifferent angles going forward, so we're looking really good t the moment. It's a great team to be part of and we're in a ood place going forward."

Brendan Rodgers added enthusiastically: "I am delighted or the football club. It's about six months and a week since came in. We talked about what we wanted to achieve and ıow we wanted to do it. We are certainly well on our way to loing that. I was very pleased with the performance.

"It's something tangible to show for our efforts. Everyone ıas talked about the great start and the great football, but ou want something to show for it. This was out first chance nd I felt the players were magnificent. For me, my job is to nanage and bring success to Celtic. I am proud to be here as nanager and to bring a trophy to the people I love, to the lub, to the support and the players.

"It's a huge privilege to be the manager at Celtic and to ıave the first trophy with my own people is very special. t's a really good feeling and I am delighted for everyone. t's great for the confidence and sets us up very well. We ıave a huge job here to sustain this and build on it. But t this moment in time, after six months, it's a great ıchievement."

Celtic had to wait until the fading moments to seal their -0 triumph over Rangers in the semi-final when Moussa Dembele struck with a neat back-heel after some great work lone by Leigh Griffiths on the right flank.

Rodgers, who reached the Final of a national Cup ompeitition for the first time in his managerial career, ıcclaimed his team's performance and said: "In order to ubber stamp that development, you want to get trophies.

League Cup Results

August 10, 2016: Last 16:
CELTIC 5 Rogic (2), Dembele (2,1 pen), Sinclair
MOTHERWELL 0
Gordon; Janko (sub: Ralston), Lustig (sub: McCart), O'Connell, Izaguirre; Brown (sub: Henderson), McGregor; Forrest, Rogic, Sinclair; Dembele.

September 21: Quarter-Final:
CELTIC 2 Forrest, Dembele
ALLOA 0
Gordon; Lustig, Toure, Simunovic (sub: Christie), Tierney; Brown, Armstrong; Roberts (sub: Sinclair), Rogic (sub: Sviatchenko), Forrest; Dembele.

October 23: Semi-Final:
CELTIC 1 Dembele
RANGERS 0
Gordon; Lustig, Simunovic, Sviatchenko, Tierney; Brown, Bitton (sub: Armstrong); Forrest (sub: Gamboa), Rogic (sub: Griffiths), Sinclair; Dembele.

November 27: Final:
CELTIC 3 Rogic, Forrest, Dembele (pen)
ABERDEEN 0
Gordon; Lustig, Simunovic, Sviatchneko, Izaguirre; Brown, Rogic (sub: McGregor); Roberts (sub: Bitton), Armstrong, Forrest (sub: Griffiths); Dembele.

"There are areas I want to improve in over time, but the players are performing magnificently well, they have that hunger to succeed and they're playing the game at a real top-level tempo, with and without the ball.

"We were very dominant in terms of chances and the power and strength of our game."

Unfortunately for Aberdeen, Celtic took those qualities into the Final the following month when they had the last say. ■

SEMI-FINAL HERO... Moussa Dembele puts Rangers to the sword – again!

Heavens Above!

CELTIC 2 ABERDEEN 1 (May 27, 2017)

Thunderous applause for Rogic's Cup winner

GOING DOWN A STORM...Tom Rogic after his late winner.

A MIGHTY thunderclap boomed over Hampden at the precise moment Tom Rogic slid the ball between Aberdeen keeper Joe Lewis and his near post to seal Celtic's first treble in sixteen years.

As the ball smacked off the back of the net, the tumultuous, crackling crescendo heralded the magical moment from the Wizard of Oz whose tantalising footwork had carved open the back-tracking rearguard as a nerve-riddled confrontation edged two minutes into stoppage time with an exhausting period of extra-time looming.

The sun had shone through the clouds at the kick-off for the Scottish Cup Final on the Saturday afternoon of May 27, 2017, but, as an enthralling encounter was played out at the national stadium in the Mount Florida district of Glasgow, the wayward and changeable weather conditions merely added to the drama and unpredictability of a tense occasion.

The contest had not started well for the champions. In the ninth minute, a corner-kick was swept in from the right by Niall McGinn and his swirling cross eliminated Jozo Simunovic and Mikael Lustig as it carried on to the inrushing Jonny Hayes, who escaped the attention of an unawares Leigh Griffiths, and the Republic of Ireland international winger caught it perfectly on the drop with his left foot. He belted an unstoppable effort beyond the exposed and alarmed Craig Gordon. Kieran Tierney's goal-line heroics in an attempt to deflect the shot went unrewarded.

It was all-square within two minutes when Callum McGregor, cutting in from the right, shrugged off a couple of rugged challenges to present a pass in front of Stuart Armstrong and the smooth midfielder provided the perfect response with the equaliser, rifling a low left-foot drive from the edge of the box across the sprawling Lewis and into the far corner.

As the minutes ticked away, referee Bobby Madden was already looking at his watch with the scoreline still deadlocked at one goal apiece. Celtic had incessantly

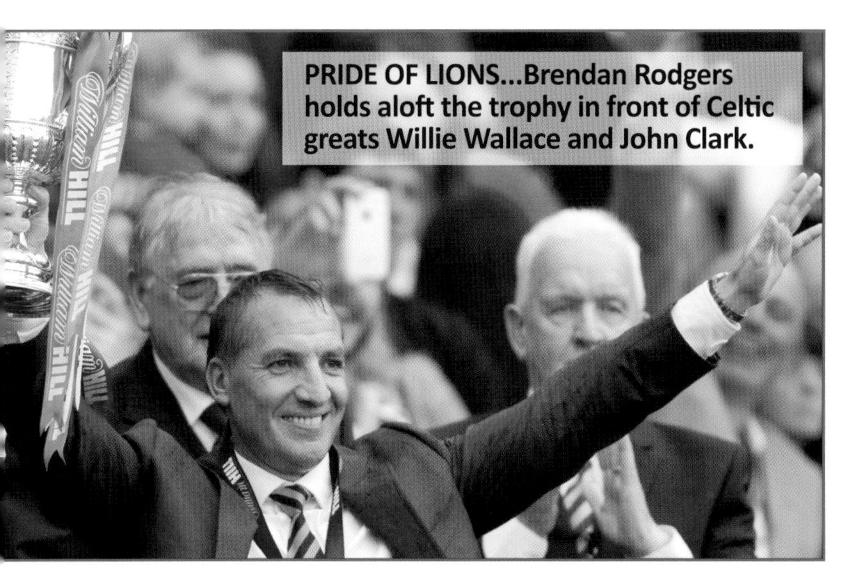
PRIDE OF LIONS...Brendan Rodgers holds aloft the trophy in front of Celtic greats Willie Wallace and John Clark.

PRIZE GUY...matchwinner Tom Rogic with the silverware.

BHOY, OH BHOY...Celtic celebrate their first domestic treble in sixteen years.

GRAND FINALE...triumphant Celts show their delight following the late dramatic win over Dons.

SCOTTISH CUP CAMPAIGN

WELL CLEARED...Scott Brown leads the charge to head away from Rangers' Danny Wilson.

PICK IT OUT... Scott Sinclair after his spot-kick success.

HAMPDEN HERE WE COME...Stuart Armstrong in action against Albion Rovers in the opening round of the Cup.

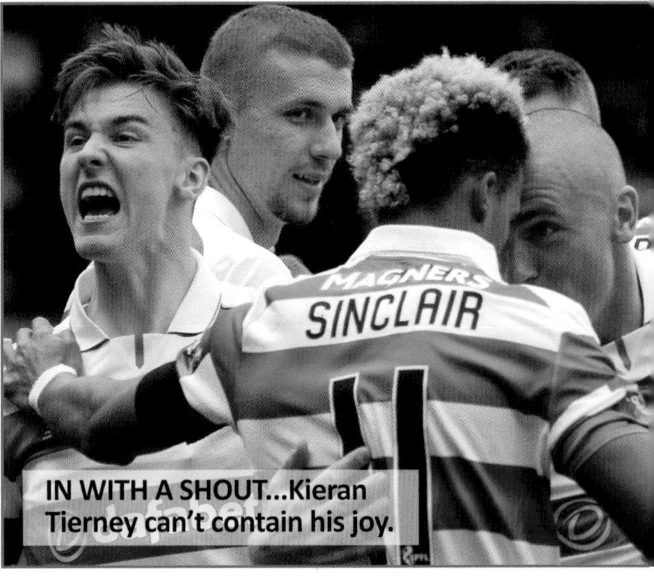

IN WITH A SHOUT...Kieran Tierney can't contain his joy.

BY THE RIGHT...Scott Sinclair prepares to sink his penalty-kick with James Tavernier looking apprehensive.

attered away at the Dons rearguard since the turnaround, but ewis, with some fine saves and courageous defending from is colleagues in front of him, had yet to yield a second goal.

And then the lean and languid figure of Rogic came iarply into focus, dancing menacingly towards the anger zone. Brendan Rodgers called the Australian player The Magic Man" and the Canberra-born personality ecided to live up to his manager's boast. No threat was nminent as he eased with nonchalant grace onto a pass om Armstrong.

He ambled forward before an unexpected spurt of cceleration saw him weave away from Anthony O'Connor s he carried into the penalty area. A shimmy of the hips ummoxed Andy Considine before the Aussie playmaker pied a vulnerable spot between Lewis and his near upright. hat was all he needed as he carefully placed the ball into the iviting area.

Nature's forces combined to applaud the individualistic ffort and the Scottish Cup was on its way to the east end f Glasgow to keep the Premiership and the League Cup ompany in the Celtic Park trophy cabinet. An extraordinary ndefeated campaign had been completed.

History had been made with virtually the last kick of the all.

The unassuming Rogic reflected afterwards: "Scoring that oal? It's hard to put into words. I picked up the ball and just ied to be positive, the space opened up for me and it was a ery special moment.

"It's not about me, but the goal was something you dream f. It's been a long season. To do what we have done in going nbeaten, winning the treble on the last day of the season in ie last minute it was an unbelievable moment for veryone."

Former Liverpool manager Rodgers, who had replaced Iorwegian Ronny Deila the previous April, was drenched s he stood on the touchline while his players cavorted with lee. In his first campaign, the Irishman had led the club to forty-seven game unbeaten sequence against Scottish pposition earning his team the tag The Invincibles.

As the raindrops cascaded from the heavens, he said: We've created an identity this season and, hopefully, we an build on that and improve over the coming years. What e have achieved has been really spectacular.

"Maybe the stars were aligned this year. I remember the entenary Year for Celtic and there's just a feeling about this eason. But don't get me wrong, we've had to earn it. We've orked hard.

"It's a huge honour. I think what the players have chieved and you see how difficult it is, the great history of iis club and the great managers and players who have been ere before me.

"To have achieved that in the first season, along with verything else that we've done is very humbling.

"I still get a wee bit of a funny feeling, it doesn't sit quite ght with me. Jock Stein was a real pioneer in leading the lub where they wanted to go. Martin O'Neill did an icredible job here.

"History will judge me and I've only just begun, so when leave here people will look at what I did. It's been truly njoyable. It's a really special feeling today."

Celtic coasted through to the semi-finals of the national competition with victories over Albion Rovers, Inverness Caley Thistle and St Mirren, scoring thirteen goals in the process and surrendering one. That set up an intriguing last-four meeting with Rangers at Hampden on the afternoon of April 23.

A cute Callum McGregor strike in the tenth minute and a Scott Sinclair penalty-kick, awarded in the fiftieth minute after James Tavernier had flattened Leigh Griffiths, were enough to send the Ibrox side, with Portuguese coach Pedro Caixinha in charge, toppling towards oblivion in a one-sided contest.

A delighted Rodgers looked ahead to the showpiece showdown with Aberdeen and said: "Our plan is to win games and we find ways to do that.

"We're one game away from a really historic season."

However, even the Celtic manager could not have scripted the heartsopping events at the national stadium before the glittering prize was handed over to his Invincibles. ■

Scottish Cup Results

January 22, 2017:
Fourth Round:
ALBION ROVERS 0
CELTIC 3 Sinclair, Dembele, Armstrong
Gordon; Gamboa, Lustig (sub: Simunovic), Boyata, Tierney (sub: McGregor); Brown, Bitton; Forrest (sub: Roberts), Armstrong, Sinclair; Dembele.

February 11:
Fifth Round:
CELTIC 6 Lustig, Dembele (3), Tierney, Brown
INVERNESS CALEY THISTLE 0
Gordon; Lustig, Boyata (sub: Toure), Sviatchenko, Tierney; Brown, Bitton; Forrest, Henderson (sub: McGregor), Sinclair; Dembele (sub: Ciftci).

March 5:
Quarter-Final:
CELTIC 4 Lustig, Sinclair, Dembele, Griffiths
ST MIRREN 1 Davis
Gordon; Lustig, Boyata, Sviatchenko, Tierney; Brown, Bitton (sub: Griffiths); Mackay-Steven (sub: Roberts), Armstrong (sub: Kouassi), Sinclair; Dembele.

April 23:
Semi-Final:
CELTIC 2 McGregor, Sinclair (pen)
RANGERS 0
Gordon; Lustig, Simunovic, Boyata, Tierney; Brown, Armstrong; Roberts (sub: Forrest), McGregor (sub: Rogic), Sinclair; Dembele (sub: Griffiths).

May 27:
Final:
CELTIC 2 Armstrong, Rogic
ABERDEEN 1 Hayes
Gordon; Lustig, Simunovic, Boyata, Tierney (sub: Rogic); Brown, Armstrong; Roberts (sub: Sviatchenko), McGregor, Sinclair; Griffiths.

Magnificent Seven

Rodgers so proud of his Bhoys

DEADLY DEDRYCK...Belgian defender Boyata is congratulated by his Celtic colleagues after a superb goal against Hearts.

CELTIC brought down the curtain on a seventh successive title triumph with the loss of a proud FIFTY-SIX game unbeaten sequence at Parkhead when Aberdeen won 1-0 on May 13 2018.

And no-one in the 60,000 sell-out crowd appeared to be too perturbed by the change of circumstances.

The crown was about to be passed to skipper Scott Brown following another championship triumph and the fans were in a party mood on Flag Day in the east end of Glasgow.

Prior to the reverse against Derek McInnes' side, the last time the Hoops had sampled defeat on their home soil was on December 19, 2015 when Motherwell won 2-1. On that occasion, Mark McGhee's Fir Park outfit came back from Nir Bitton's opener to score twice through Louis Moult – the deciding goal coming from the penalty spot – for their first victory at Celtic Park for nearly eight years.

The loss meant Ronny Deila's team had gone four games without a win on home turf – the worst run since Tony Mowbray was manager in season 2009/10. Ajax (2-1) and Molde (2-1) both won their Europa League ties and Kilmarnock forced a goalless draw in the league. Despite that loss, Celtic remained top of the title by a point from the chasing Pittodrie team.

They unfurled their fifth successive Premiership flag at the end of the campaign as they exacted revenge on Well with a 7-0 trouncing in Deila's last game on May 15, 2016.

Brendan Rodgers witnessed his team drawing only two home games in his debut 2016/17 season, both ending in 1-1 stalemates, against Rangers in March and Partick Thistle the following month.

This time around, they had been held seven times – twice by Kilmarnock (1-1 and 0-0), St Johnstone (1-1 and 0-0), Hibs (2-2), Rangers (0-0) and Dundee (0-0).

NATIONAL TREASURE... Brendan Rodgers proudly holds aloft the newly-won League Cup at Hampden following the 2-0 triumph over Motherwell in November.

Scottish Premier League Table

P	Team	Pld	W	D	L	GF	GA	GD	Pts
1	**Celtic - Champions**	**38**	**24**	**10**	**4**	**73**	**25**	**+48**	**82**
2	Aberdeen	38	22	7	9	56	37	+19	73
3	Rangers	38	21	7	10	76	50	+26	70
4	Hibernian	38	18	13	7	62	46	+16	67
5	Kilmarnock	38	16	11	11	49	47	+2	59
6	Heart of Midlothian	38	12	13	13	39	39	0	49
7	Motherwell	38	13	9	16	43	49	-6	48
8	St Johnstone	38	12	10	16	42	53	-11	46
9	Dundee	38	11	6	21	36	59	-23	39
10	Hamilton	38	9	6	23	47	66	-19	33
11	Partick Thistle	38	8	9	20	31	62	-31	33
12	Ross County	38	6	11	21	40	62	-22	29

League Cup Final

November 26, 2017:

CELTIC 2 Forrest, Dembele (pen)
MOTHERWELL 0

Gordon; Lustig, Simunovic, Boyata, Tierney; Brown, Armstrong; Forrest (sub: Roberts), McGregor (sub: Rogic), Sinclair; Dembele (sub: Griffiths).

Scottish Cup Final

May 19, 2018: **CELTIC 2** McGregor, Ntcham
MOTHERWELL 0

Gordon; Lustig, Boyata, Ajer (sub: Simunovic), Tierney; Brown, Ntcham; Forrest (sub: Sinclair), Rogic (sub: Armstrong), McGregor; Dembele.

HEAVENS ABOVE...Dedryk Boyata celebrates a goal at Tynecastle.

MASTER MARKSMAN... Leigh Griffiths after another strike.

SCREAM AND SHOUT... Mikael Lustig has his say.

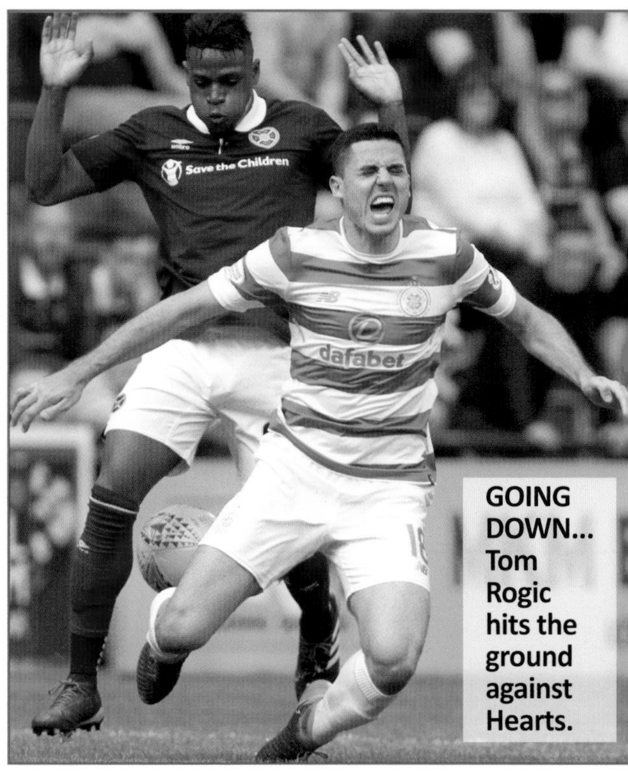

GOING DOWN... Tom Rogic hits the ground against Hearts.

TRICKS AND FLICKS...Odsonne Edouard, watched by keeper Trevor Carson, piles on the pressure at Fir Park.

And the setback against the Dons was the first time the ishman had sampled defeat in Glasgow.

But the loss to Andy Considine's goal failed to put a ampener on the celebrations and captain Scott Brown, ho played a major role in all seven successes, insisted inning the Premiership just gets sweeter.

The all-action midfielder admitted: "Every year it gets ore special and more emotional, especially doing seven a row. It's amazing, to be perfectly honest.

"We let ourselves down a little bit on this occasion, but, the end of the day, we'd already won the title. It was ways going to be hard to do the exact same as we did last ason, but we keep winning trophies.

"We've played SIXTY games so far this season and we ep pushing at this level.

"Those big games and big occasions, we need to make re we turn up and we have done in the past."

Brendan Rodgers was disappointed with the result and admitted "the team with the greater need got the result".

He added: "It's the bigger picture for us and I can't forget the work the players have done – you enter a league to win it and they have done that. I'm delighted.

"In my first season, we won it in the best way we possibly could. We didn't quite match that this year, but in the big games, the players have produced and it's great credit to them.

"It's important to celebrate today, but we focus on next week's Scottish Cup Final and, hopefully, we can finish off a remarkable season.

"There were lots of performances – the recent game against Rangers will live long in the memory as it capped off a great campaign for us."

Fans' favourite Kieran Tierney added: "Being a lifelong Celtic supporter, to celebrate in front of the fans is a dream come true for me.

BY THE RIGHT...Moussa Dembele sweeps a shot past Hearts keeper Jon McLaughlin.

WOE...Dembele looks unhappy after miss.

SKY'S THE LIMIT...Dembele shows his joy after a strike.

CRASH...French ace fires in a shot against Well.

NICE ONE...Dembele flicks in a goal against St. Johnstone keeper Zander Clark.

HUSH...Scott Sinclair makes his point after scoring.

EAR WE GO...Sinclair after scoring.

CLAP HANDS...Sinclair shows his appreciation.

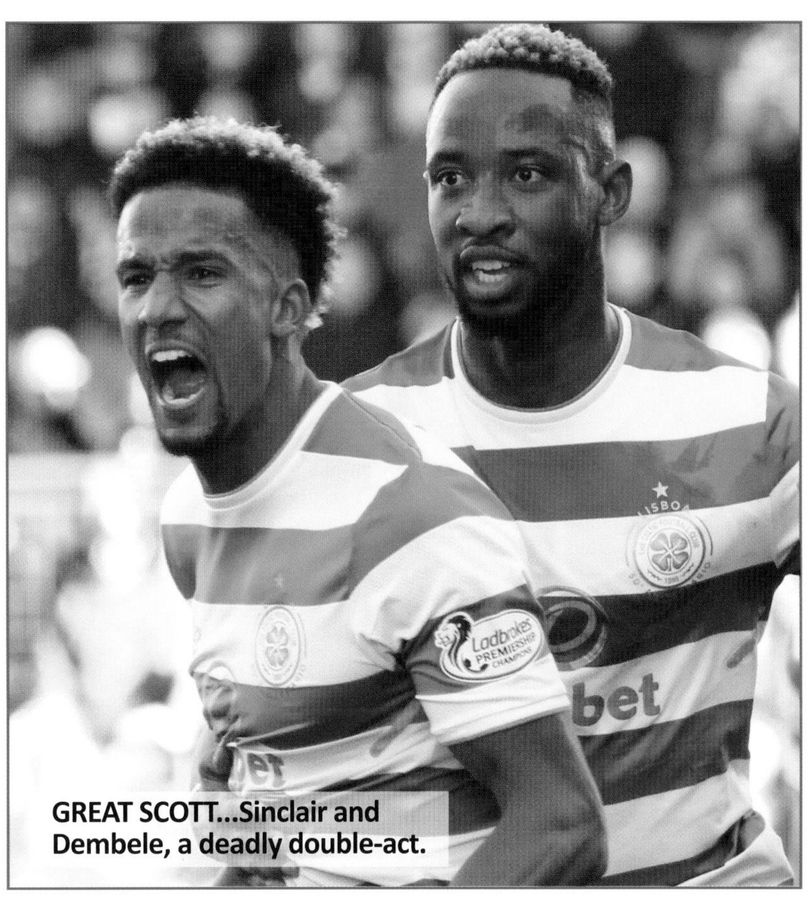

GREAT SCOTT...Sinclair and Dembele, a deadly double-act.

SPOT-KICK SUCCESS... Sinclair scores at Fir Park.

HIB HIB HOORAY... Sinclair demonstrates his joy after netting at Easter Road.

LETHAL LEIGH...Celtic striker Griffiths is in full flow, but is thwarted on this occasion by the Dundee goalkeeper at Dens Park.

"It's been a great season and I'm delighted. There's no words to describe it, I'm so grateful to every single fan for the support they have given me and I try my best to repay it."

Undoubtedly, the highlight of the Premiership campaign was the 5-0 thrashing of Rangers at Parkhead on April 29, the afternoon where the team secured their seventh title on the spin with a pulverising performance that dismantled their opponents.

The unstoppable Odsonne Edouard notched two and James Forrest contributed another with a classy finish after a serpentine run through the defence to hand the champions a three-goal interval advantage. Tom Rogic and Callum McGregor added two more shortly after the interval and, with half-an-hour still to play, the Hoops could have gone for a record-breaking score against their Glasgow neighbours.

Overworked keeper Jak Alnwick made three excellent second-half saves during a torrid spell as the green-and-white legions threatened to sweep their rivals out of the ground. This was a humiliation for the visitors who, coincidentally, lost 5-1 to Celtic on their own ground in another rout.

Rodgers' rampaging team went ahead in the fourteenth minute when Kieran Tierney raced away from Daniel Candeias on the right and set up Edouard to slide a close-range effort beyond Alnwick. The second goal duly arrived for the Frenchman when he collected a pass from Forrest and shot across the keeper into the corner.

A third arrived before the break. Dedryck Boyata won possession and released Forrest who zipped inside one challenge, hared between two flummoxed opponents and smashed an angled drive low into the rigging.

After the restart, Celtic maintained the awesome pressure and Alnwick saved well from McGregor, but the ball was

HEADS I WIN...Leigh Griffiths demonstrates his striking ability as he gets on the end of a Scott Sinclair cross.

IN YOU GO...the Hamilton Accies keeper is helpless as the ball arrows in on its target.

IN THE NET...Griffiths turns around to see the result of his penalty-box prowess.

ALL SMILES...skipper supreme Scott Brown celebrates with the fans after another triumph.

ON THE RUN...flying winger James Forrest leaves Kilmarnock midfielder Youssouf Mulumbu in his wake.

orked back to Rogic and the Australian, almost lazily, swept left-foot effort into the exposed net. The fifth came soon ter when Edouard casually sidestepped James Tavernier nd delivered a pass to McGregor who put it away for his eventh strike of the season. Cue more rejoicing.

Brendan Rodgers insisted Rangers got off lightly with his am five goals ahead with thirty-seven minutes still to play.

The Celtic boss remarked: "We're about running hard, st and aggressive and when we do that we give ourselves chance to create lots of opportunities. We scored five and was probably going on seven or eight; their keeper made ome great saves.

"It's a great tribute to the work of the players, the scrutiny ey are under to perform like that. We should have had ven, but we'll take five.

"We obviously know the consequence of the game and all e historical facts around it, Celtic to win the title here against Rangers for the first time in thirty-nine years, but I said to the players: 'You've got to play football'.

"Our basic rules were very simple. It was to attack with real aggression and intensity, try and recover the ball as quick as we can when we lose it and when we can't do that then make sure you are tight and compact and look to dominate as much of the ball as you can and give it your best shot.

"I don't think I could have asked any more of the players, they were absolutely brilliant. I'm really proud."

That is why there wasn't too much distress when Andy Considine's six-yard effort escaped Scott Bain at his right-hand post two minutes after the restart of the last Premiership game of the season on May 13.

The hard work had been done in the previous thirty-seven games to make sure the Magnificent Seven was already heading for the Celtic trophy cabinet. ■

Premiership Results

August 5, 2017: **CELTIC 4** Griffiths (2), Sinclair, McGregor
HEARTS 1 Goncalves
Gordon; Lustig, Bitton, Simunovic, Tierney; Brown, Ntcham (sub: Armstrong); Forrest, McGregor (sub: Rogic), Sinclair; Griffiths (sub: Hayes).

August 11: **PARTICK THISTLE 0**
CELTIC 1 Ntcham
Gordon; Lustig, Simunovic, Bitton, Tierney; Brown, Ntcham (sub: Armstrong); Hayes (sub: Griffiths), McGregor (sub: Rogic), Sinclair; Forrest.

August 19: **KILMARNOCK 0**
CELTIC 2 Forrest, McGregor
Gordon; Ralston, Ajer, Tierney (sub: Bitton), Miller; Brown, Armstrong; McGregor, Rogic, Benyu (sub: Lustig); Forrest (sub: Griffiths).

August 26: **CELTIC 1** McGregor
ST JOHNSTONE 1 MacLean
Gordon; Ralston (sub: McGregor), Lustig, Bitton, Tierney; Brown, Ntcham (sub: Armstrong); Forrest (sub: Hayes), Rogic, Sinclair; Griffiths.

September 8: **HAMILTON ACCIES 1** Gogic
CELTIC 4 Armstrong, Sinclair (2), Edouard
Gordon; Lustig, Simunovic (sub: Bitton), Tierney; Brown, Armstrong (sub: Ntcham); Forrest, McGregor, Roberts (sub: Hayes); Edouard, Sinclair.

September 16: **CELTIC 4** Rogic, Dembele, Forrest (2)
ROSS COUNTY 0
Gordon; Ralston, Simunovic, Bitton; Brown, Armstrong (sub: McGregor); Forrest, Rogic, Hayes; Dembele (sub: Edouard), Griffiths (sub: Sinclair).

September 23: **RANGERS 0**
CELTIC 2 Rogic, Griffiths
Gordon; Lustig, Simunovic, Boyata, Tierney; Brown, Armstrong; Roberts (sub: Forrest), Rogic (sub: McGregor), Sinclair; Griffiths (sub: Dembele).

September 30: **CELTIC 2** McGregor (2)
HIBS 2 McGinn (2)
Gordon; Lustig, Boyata, Tierney; Forrest (sub: Roberts), Ntcham, McGregor, Rogic, Hayes; Dembele (sub: Griffiths), Edouard (sub: Sinclair)

October 14: **CELTIC 1** Ntcham
DUNDEE 0
De Vries; Gamboa (sub: Ajer), Bitton, Boyata, Tierney; Ntcham, Kouassi (sub: L Henderson); Roberts, McGregor, Sinclair; Griffiths (sub: Dembele).

October 25: **ABERDEEN 0**
CELTIC 3 Tierney, Dembele (2)
Gordon; Lustig, Bitton, Boyata, Tierney; Brown, Armstrong; Forrest (sub: Hayes), Rogic (sub: Sinclair), McGregor; Dembele (sub: Griffiths

October 28: **CELTIC 1** Griffiths
KILMARNOCK 1 Jones
Gordon; Lustig, Bitton, Ajer, Tierney; Ntcham (sub: Armstrong), Kouass Roberts (sub: Sinclair), Rogic, Johnston (sub: Dembele); Griffiths.

November 4: **ST JOHNSTONE 0**
CELTIC 4 Sinclair, Dembele, Anderson (og), Ntcham
Gordon; Lustig, Boyata, Bitton, Tierney; Brown, Armstrong (sub: Ntcham); Forrest (sub: Hayes), McGregor (sub: Rogic), Sinclair; Dembele.

November 18: **ROSS COUNTY 0**
CELTIC 1 Griffiths
Gordon; Lustig, Boyata, Bitton, Tierney; Brown, Armstrong; Forrest (sub: Hayes), McGregor (sub: Griffiths), Sinclair; Dembele (sub: Ntcham).

November 29: **MOTHERWELL 1** Lustig (og)
CELTIC 1 Sinclair (pen)
Gordon; Lustig (sub: Edouard), Ajer, Boyata, Tierney; Brown, Armstrong (sub: Sinclair); Roberts (sub: Rogic), McGregor, Forrest; Griffiths.

December 2: **CELTIC 5** Edouard (3), Forrest (2)
MOTHERWELL 1 Frear
Gordon: Lustig, Ajer, Boyata, Tierney; Brown, Ntcham (sub: McGregor); Hayes (sub: Forrest), Rogic, Sinclair (sub: Armstrong); Edouard.

December 10: **HIBS 2** Ambrose, Shaw
CELTIC 2 Sinclair (2)
Gordon; Lustig, Simunovic, Boyata, Tierney; Brown, Ntcham (sub: Armstrong); Forrest (sub: Hayes), McGregor, Sinclair; Edouard (sub: Dembele).

December 13: **CELTIC 3** Ntcham, Forrest, Sinclair
HAMILTON ACCIES 1 Redmond
Gordon; Ajer, Bitton, Boyata (sub: Simunovic); Brown, McGregor. Ntcham, Armstrong; Forrest (sub: Hayes), Edouards (sub: Griffiths), Sinclair.

December 17: **HEARTS 4** Cochrane, Lafferty, Milinkovic (2,1pen)
CELTIC 0
Gordon; Lustig, Simunovic, Boyata, Tierney (sub: Armstrong); Brown Ntcham (sub: Dembele); Forrest, McGregor (sub: Edouard), Sinclair; Griffiths.

SEASON 2017/2018

ecember 20: **CELTIC 2** Armstrong, Tierney
PARTICK THISTLE 0
ordon; Lustig, Ajer, Boyata, Tierney; Brown, Armstrong; Forrest
ub: Hayes), McGregor, Sinclair (sub: Johnston); Edouard (sub: Griffiths).

ecember 23: **CELTIC 3** Lustig, Hayes, Ntcham
ABERDEEN 0
ordon; Lustig, Ajer, Boyata, Tierney; Brown, Armstrong; Hayes (sub:
cGregor), Ntcham, Sinclair (sub: Forrest); Dembele (sub: Edouard).

ecember 26: **DUNDEE 0**
CELTIC 2 Forrest, Griffiths
ordon; Lustig, Boyata, Ajer, Tierney; Brown, Ntcham
ub: Armstrong); Hayes (sub: Johnston), McGregor, Forrest;
iffiths (sub: Dembele).

ecember 30: **CELTIC 0**
RANGERS 0
ordon; Lustig, Boyata, Ajer, Tierney; Brown, Armstrong; Forrest,
cGregor, Sinclair (sub: Ntcham); Dembele (sub: Griffiths).

nuary 23, 2018:
PARTICK THISTLE 1 Sammon (pen)
CELTIC 2 Sinclair (pen), Griffiths
ordon; Lustig (sub: Griffiths), Boyata, Ajer, Tierney; Brown, Ntcham;
rrest, McGregor, Sinclair (sub: Simunovic); Edouard (sub: Bitton).

nuary 27: **CELTIC 1** Griffiths
HIBS 0
ordon (sub: De Vries); Boyata, Simunovic, Ajer; Brown, Ntcham,
erney; Forrest (sub: Kouassi), McGregor, Sinclair; Griffiths
ub: Dembele).

nuary 30: **CELTIC 3** Edouard, Boyata, Dembele
HEARTS 1 Lafferty
e Vries; Ajer, Simunovic, Boyata; Brown, Kouassi, Tierney; Forrest
ub: Musonda), Ntcham, Edouard (sub: McGregor); Dembele
ub: Sinclair).

ebruary 3: **KILMARNOCK 1** Mulumbu
CELTIC 0
e Vries; Hendry, Boyata (sub: Bitton), Ajer (sub: Sinclair); Brown,
uassi (sub: Edouard), Tierney; Forrest, Musonda, Ntcham; Dembele.

ebruary 18: **CELTIC 0**
ST JOHNSTONE 0
e Vries; Gamboa, Hendry, Ajer, Miller (sub: Tierney); Kouassi,
usonda, McGregor, Rogic (sub: Forrest), Sinclair; Edouard
ub: Dembele).

ebruary 25: **ABERDEEN 0**
CELTIC 2 Dembele, Tierney
e Vries; Lustig, Ajer, Simunovic, Tierney; Brown, Ntcham; Forrest
ub: Hendry), Rogic (sub: McGregor), Sinclair (sub: Edouard); Dembele.

larch 11: **RANGERS 2** Windass, Candieas
CELTIC 3 Rogic, Dembele, Edouard
in; Boyata, Ajer, Simunovic, Tierney; Brown, Ntcham; Forrest (sub:
douard), Rogic (sub: Hendry), McGregor; Dembele (sub: Armstrong).

March 18: **MOTHERWELL 0**
CELTIC 0
Bain; Hendry, Boyata, Ajer; Brown, Ntcham (sub: Armstrong); Forrest
(sub: Roberts), Rogic, McGregor; Edouard (sub: Sinclair), Dembele.

March 31: **CELTIC 3** Dembele (pen), Armstrong, Rogic
ROSS COUNTY 0
Bain; Lustig, Boyata (sub: Hendry), Ajer, McGregor; Brown, Armstrong;
Forrest (sub: Roberts), Rogic, Sinclair; Dembele (sub: Griffiths).

April 4: **CELTIC 0**
DUNDEE 0
Gordon; Lustig, Hendry, Boyata, McGregor; Brown, Armstrong;
Forrest, Rogic (sub: Ntcham), Sinclair (sub: Edouard); Dembele
(sub: Griffiths).

April 8: **HAMILTON ACCIES 1** Bingham
CELTIC 2 McGregor, Griffiths
Bain; Hendry (sub: Griffiths), Boyata, Ajer, Tierney; Brown, Ntcham;
Roberts (sub: Musonda), McGregor, Sinclair; Dembele (sub: Edouard).

April 21: **HIBS 2** MacLaren, Slivka
CELTIC 1 Edouard
Gordon; Hendry, Ajer, Boyata; Forrest (sub: Roberts), Brown, Ntcham
(sub: Sinclair), Tierney; Rogic, McGregor; Griffiths (sub: Edouard).

April 29: **CELTIC 5** Edouard (2), Forrest, Rogic, McGregor
RANGERS 0
Gordon; Lustig (sub: Hendry), Boyata, Ajer, Tierney; Brown, Ntcham;
Forrest, Rogic (sub: Sinclair), McGregor; Edouard (sub: Griffiths).

May 6: **HEARTS 1** Lafferty
CELTIC 3 Boyata, Dembele, Sinclair
Bain; Lustig, Boyata, Ajer; Brown, Ntcham; Forrest, Rogic (sub: Roberts),
Edouard (sub: Sinclair), McGregor; Dembele (sub: Armstrong).

May 9: **CELTIC 0**
KILMARNOCK 0
Bain; Hendry, Simunovic, Ajer, Miller (sub: Tierney); Brown,
Armstrong (sub: Rogic); Forrest, McGregor, Sinclair; Roberts
(sub: E Henderson).

May 13: **CELTIC 0**
ABERDEEN 1 Considine
Bain; Lustig, Boyata, Ajer, Tierney (sub: Sinclair); Brown, Ntcham
(sub: Armstrong); Forrest, Rogic, McGregor; Dembele (sub: Griffiths).

Forrest on Fire

Winger sets up four in a row

DIDN'T HE DO WELL...James Forrest races away in delight after his magical opening goal.

CELTIC 2 MOTHERWELL 0 (November 26, 2017)

BRENDAN RODGERS became the first Celtic manager since the legendary Jock Stein to win four successive domestic trophies as the Hoops beat Motherwell 2-0 in the League Cup Final on November 26, 2017.

The Irishman's side had to battle all the way to overcome a stubborn and gallant Fir Park outfit who eventually succumbed when James Forrest curled an unstoppable effort beyond the stranded Trevor Carson shortly after the restart.

It was the Scotland international winger's third goal in three Finals in the competition.

Craig Gordon was forced to make a phenomenal reflex save to thwart an acrobatic close-range header from Louis Moult which the agile keeper diverted onto the crossbar on its way to safety.

Well's hopes ended when rugged centre-half Cedric Kipr was red-carded following a foul on Scott Sinclair that sent the English raider spinning in the box. Referee Craig Thomson banished the defender and Moussa Dembele effectively ended the game as a contest when he rolled the penalty-kick into the corner of the net with Carson again helpless.

Stephen Robinson's side never looked like preventing

HAMPDEN HEROES... Celtic players celebrate with the glittering prize.

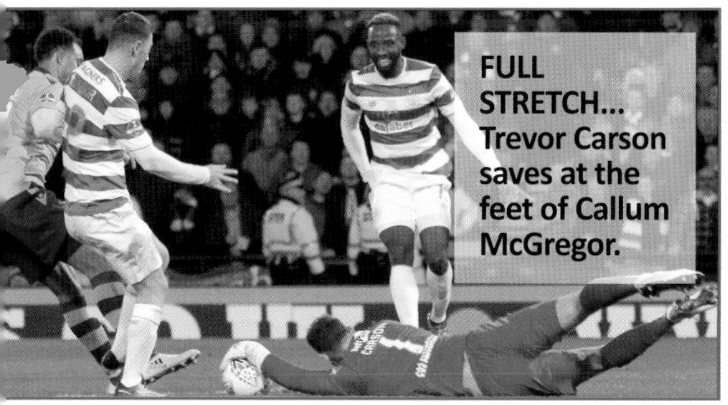

FULL STRETCH... Trevor Carson saves at the feet of Callum McGregor.

ON THE SPOT...Moussa Dembele nets the decisive penalty-kick against Well.

THE EYES HAVE IT...Moussa Dembele sweeps an effort beyond Hibs keeper Ross Turnbull in the 4-2 semi-final win.

LEAGUE CUP CAMPAIGN

DUNDEE DELIGHT...Scott Sinclair and Leigh Griffiths celebrate the 4-0 win at Dens Park.

THE HOOPS ROAR...Kieran Tierney urges on his team mates against Dundee.

MY BALL... Dedryk Boyata clears from Louis Moult.

SCARF ACE...Brendan Rodgers' Hampden joy.

HEAVENWARDS...Dembele looks to the skies after his second goal against Hibs.

RIGHT-BACK TO HAPPINESS...defender Mikael Lustig scores one of his two goals in the semi-final win over the Easter Road men.

st season's treble-winners clocking up a remarkable XTY-FIFTH domestic game without defeat and their venteenth victory in their thirty-second League Cup Final.

In truth, Celtic found it difficult to make any headway in e opening forty-five minutes with the smothering tactics their opponents diminishing the threats of individuals ch as Stuart Armstrong and Scott Sinclair, but Callum cGregor still managed to look dangerous while Forrest as in the mood with some darting runs on the flank.

Four minutes into the second-half, he took advantage some hesitancy in the Well defensive ranks when Charles unne and Peter Hartley gave the pacy menace some space have a pop with his left foot, Forrest was emphatic with arcing shot that perfectly curled away from the lunging rson into the far corner.

It unlocked the stuffy confrontation and there was no opping the trophy holders as they went in search of the cond killer goal. It duly arrived with the penalty-kick that as tucked away with the usual nonchalant grace of Dembele.

It was a fair response from a Celtic team that had just had e stuffing knocked out of them in the French capital. It was evening to forget and all eyes were on the holders to see w they reacted to such an embarrassment with the rest of urope looking on.

Following the seven-goal drubbing from Paris Saint-ermain in a lop-sided Champions League game, Brendan odgers praised his players as he said: "We had to tick a few aracter boxes after midweek.

"Yet again the players produced. It was always going to difficult for us, how Motherwell have started the season d the confidence they have in terms of how they play.

"Once we got the first goal, we settled into a rhythm d it's our fourth trophy in twelve months, a phenomenal hievement, really, and a huge credit to the players for their inger and desire.

"Jamesy's goal was a wonderful piece of skill, and difficult r the defender because he maybe thinks he's going to go wn the outside, but he's got that ability to come into his t side and hit it with the outside of his right foot or bend it he did with his left.

"I look at the Kipre challenge and think it's a penalty. s a great ball, Scotty makes the run and is getting there. e defender cannot get there, so he impedes him, he pulls m, so it's a penalty.

"I'm not sure what the rules are now, I'm not sure if it's sending off. I'm sure Stephen Robinson will feel it's a bit rsh being a sending off. But it's definitely a penalty.

"We managed the 11 v 10 very well. Sometimes you see it hen you're playing against the man down and you can go a loose, but our positioning was good and we broke away. e should have made the game a lot more comfortable with e chances that we had.

"My idea after midweek was just to try to get the win and ay well. The players deserve a huge amount of credit. We me back after the midweek – a sore one to take – but the lture that we created the process by which we review that ows us to come in with a real positive attitude, to work well.

"It's a trophy for everyone at the club. The support was nazing, really helping the team, the backroom staff and the ork that they put in, combined with the players." ■

League Cup Results

August 8, 2017: Second Round:
CELTIC 5 Griffiths (2, 1 pen), Ralston, Tierney, Armstrong
KILMARNOCK 0
Gordon; Ralston, Ajer, Tierney, Miller; Kouassi (sub: Ntcham), Armstrong; Hayes, Rogic, Benyu (sub: McGregor); Griffiths (sub: Forrest).

September 20: Quarter-Final:
DUNDEE 0
CELTIC 4 Sinclair (pen), Forrest (2), McGregor
Gordon; Lustig, Boyata (sub: Ralston), Bitton, Tierney; Brown, Ntcham; Roberts (sub: McGregor), Sinclair, Forrest; Griffiths (sub: Edouard).

October 21: Semi-Final:
CELTIC 4 Lustig (2), Dembele (2)
HIBS 2 Stokes (pen), Shaw
Gordon;Lustig, Boyata, Bitton, Tierney; Brown, Armstrong (sub: Rogic); Roberts (sub: Forrest), McGregor, Sinclair; Griffiths (sub: Dembele).

November 26: Final:
CELTIC 2 Forrest, Dembele (pen)
MOTHERWELL 0
Gordon; Lustig, Simunovic, Boyata, Tierney; Brown, Armstrong; Forrest (sub: Roberts), McGregor (sub: Rogic), Sinclair; Dembele (sub: Griffiths).

HAMPDEN HUGS...bosses Brendan Rodgers and Neil Lennon embrace before Celtic's 4-2 semi-final victory over Hibs.

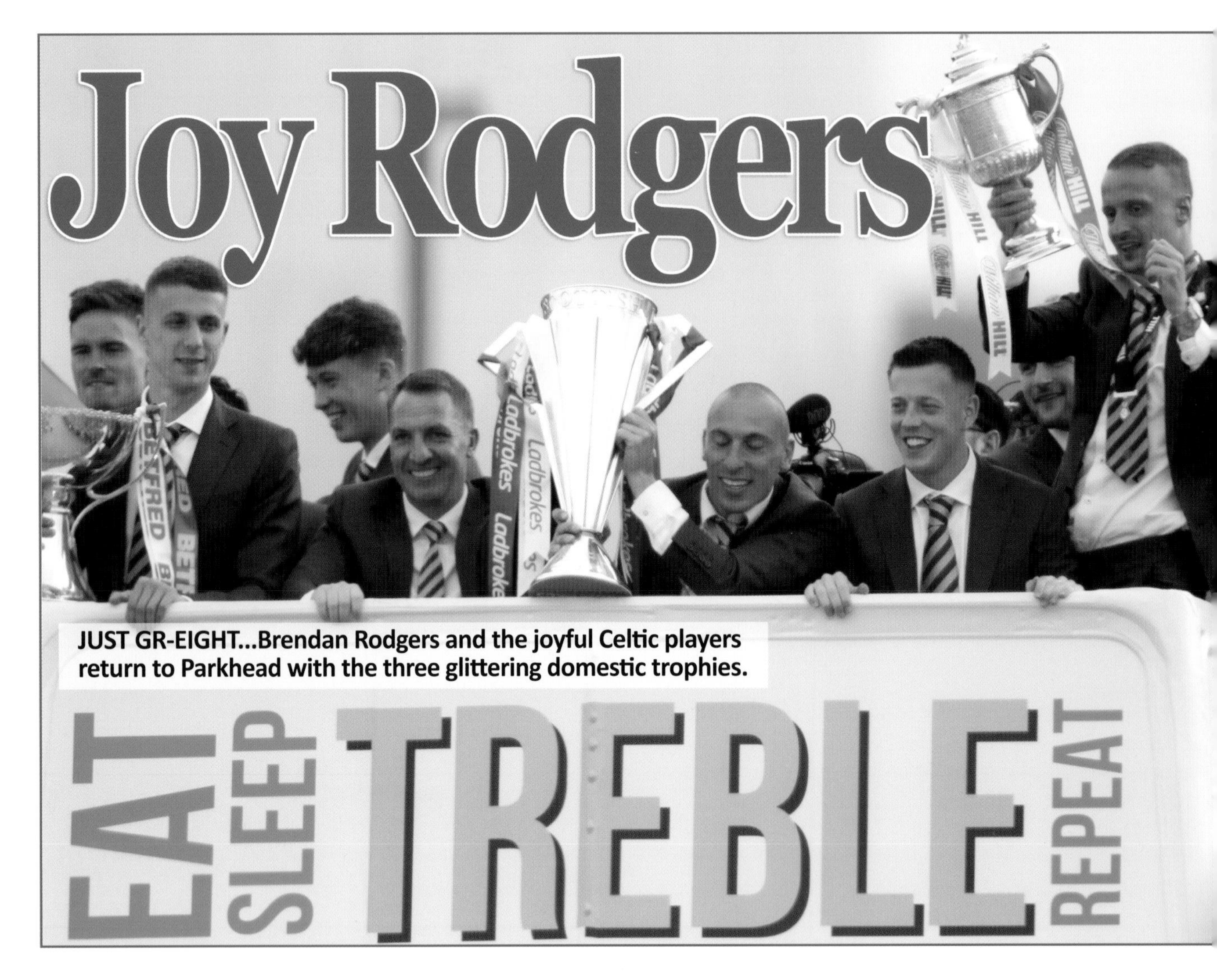

JUST GR-EIGHT...Brendan Rodgers and the joyful Celtic players return to Parkhead with the three glittering domestic trophies.

Eightsome reel for Hoops boss

CELTIC 2 MOTHERWELL 0 (May 19, 2018)

BRENDAN RODGERS enjoyed an eightsome reel at Hampden when Celtic comfortably overcame Motherwell 2-0 to win the Scottish Cup on a gloriously sunny Saturday afternoon, May 19, 2018.

In the space of two memorable years, the Irishman had transformed the national stadium from a graveyard of dreams to a Hoops fortress after taking over from Ronny Deila two years earlier.

Under the Norwegian, the team failed to progress in three domestic semi-finals – two in actual play in controversial circumstances and one on penalty-kicks.

Inverness Caley Thistle and Ross County beat 10-man Celtic teams – Craig Gordon and Efe Ambrose red-carded – while Rangers, following a 2-2 draw after extra-time, won 5-4 on spot-kicks – hastening the end of Deila's two-year reign.

Rodgers, who moved in at Parkhead within a month of that dismal display against the Ibrox Championship outfit in the Scottish Cup-tie, clocked up his EIGHTH successive victory in the historic triumph over the Fir Park outfit to claim an unprecedented double treble to send the Celtic supporters into raptures.

It was seven from heaven the previous month in the runaway 4-0 semi-final win over the Ibrox men, then managed by caretaker Graeme Murty who was sacked from his post just over two weeks later.

In the League Cup semi-final the previous season, Moussa Dembele netted in the last minute to knock out Rangers, with Mark Warburton in charge, and the French Under-21 hitman struck again in the 3-0 win over Aberdeen in the Final with Tom Rogic and James Forrest also on target.

In the Scottish Cup last-four encounter, Callum McGregor and Scott Sinclair did the damage against the Ibrox team, with Pedro Caixinha as boss, in a 2-0 success

SEASON 2017/2018

SMILES BETTER... Brendan Rodgers shows his delight.

FINAL PRIZE GUYS...back row (left to right): Craig Gordon, Moussa Dembele, James Forrest, Olivier Ntcham, Dedryck Boyata, Tom Rogic, Kristoffer Ajer; Front row: Mikael Lustig, Scott Brown, Kieran Tierney and Callum McGregor.

IT'S OURS...Scott Brown and Craig Gordon with the Cup.

JOY BHOY...Callum McGregor scores the second goal in the 4-0 semi-final rout against Rangers.

HAIL HAIL...Kieran Tierney has his say.

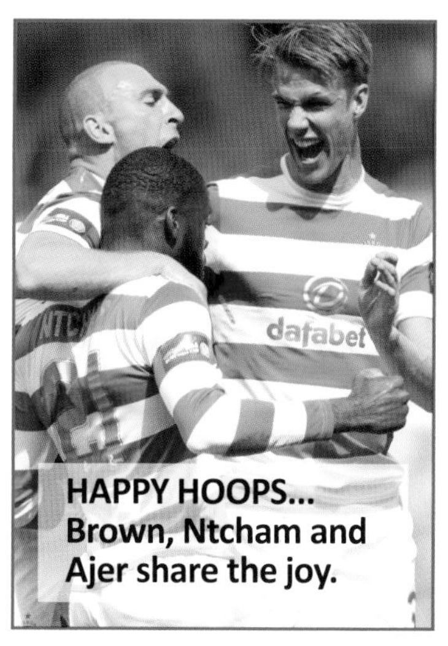

HAPPY HOOPS... Brown, Ntcham and Ajer share the joy.

ON THE RUN... Dembele takes on defender Cedric Kipre.

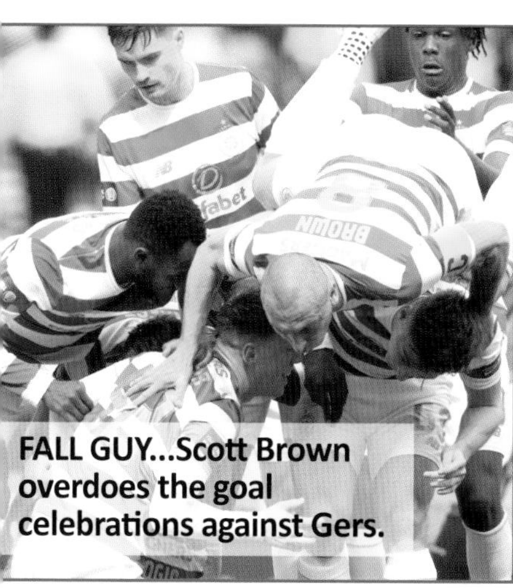

FALL GUY...Scott Brown overdoes the goal celebrations against Gers.

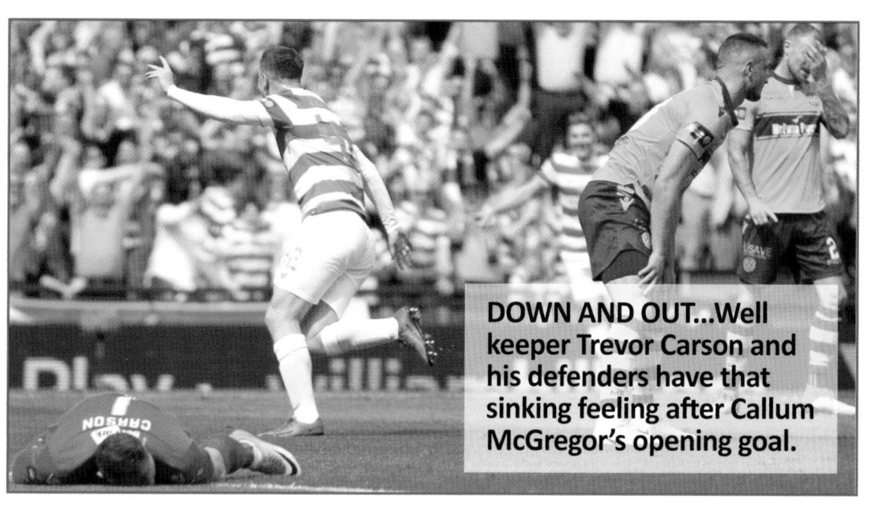

DOWN AND OUT...Well keeper Trevor Carson and his defenders have that sinking feeling after Callum McGregor's opening goal.

SCOTTISH CUP CAMPAIGN

WHAM! Olivier Ntcham (half-hidden by Chris Cadden) fires in the second goal.

AIR WE GO...the Frenchman performs an acrobatic somersault much to the surprise of Scott Brown.

FLIPPIN HECK... the Celtic skipper is still bemused.

and Stuart Armstrong and Aussie playmaker Rogic downed Aberdeen 2-1 in the Final.

In the 2017/18 campaign, Neil Lennon's gallant Hibs side were beaten 4-2 in the League Cup semi-final with Dembele (2) and Mikael Lustig (2) seeing off the challenge from Edinburgh.

James Forrest and Dembele, from the penalty spot, were the marksmen in the 2-0 victory over Motherwell as the trophy was retained.

Celtic looked unstoppable in their charge towards their Scottish Cup success and emphasised their ambitions with an utterly ruthless performance against their Ibrox foes in the semi-final when they routed a toiling Gers side by four clear goals – and it could have been even more humiliating for their opponents.

It was four going on double figures as Dembele and Co swarmed around Wes Foderingham's goalmouth in ruthless fashion and they served a warning early on when a shot on the turn from the French powerhouse frontman clattered off the woodwork and bounced to safety.

There were a couple of scares before the champions claimed the breakthrough goal in the twenty-second minute when Dembele ran in behind the defence to pull down a ball from Oliver Ntcham and lay a pass back to James Forrest who rolled it in front of Tom Rogic. The Australian playmaker, with commendable poise, swivelled away from Ross McCrorie and swished a low drive into the unprotected left-hand side of the Foderingham net.

Skipper Scott Brown and midfield cohorts Callum McGregor and Ntcham were bossing the contest and it was no surprise when Rodgers' men doubled their advantage seven minutes before the interval. Kieran Tierney crossed invitingly from the left, Russell Martin's hasty clearance fell directly to the grateful McGregor who didn't break stride as he launched a first-time right-foot drive wide of the despairing Foderingham.

It wasn't long before the Celtic choir were in full voice again in the fifty-second minute when McCrorie was red-carded following a clumsy challenge on Dembele and the French ace took the penalty-kick award with some aplomb as he cheekily dinked the ball down the middle of the goal as the keeper took off for his left. Foderingham faced another spot-kick twelve minutes from the end of an excruciating afternoon for the overrun Ibrox outfit following a foul by Jason Holt on Patrick Roberts. This time Ntcham stepped forward to drill the fourth and final goal into the bottom right-hand corner.

BHOYS ZONE

JAMES FORREST scored his first-ever hat-trick in Celtic's 3-2 Scottish Cup fifth round win over Partick Thistle at Parkhead on February 8, 2018. Last season the Scotland International winger went one better in the Hoops' 6-0 Premiership triumph over St. Johnstone in Perth on October 7 – all four goals coming in the first-half.

A beaming Rodgers exclaimed: "I'm always looking to push the players and bring out that bit more from them, that makes a difference going into these big games and they bring the real edge to it.

"They have really inspired the supporters in my time here, the supporters feel safe that the players are going to give everything they can. We have a way of playing that we know can win games. I thought we controlled the game well in the first-half. We played around their shape. Rangers looked like they were trying to block the middle of the pitch, but that allowed us to exploit the sides.

"We had fairly decent control without too much threat against us. The team was compact, defending well, counter-pressing well and we get a very good first goal that relaxes you as well, a brilliant finish from Tom Rogic, a wonderful piece of skill. From there we had really good control throughout the game."

And the Celtic manager was equally delighted the following month after the historic 2-0 triumph over Motherwell in the showpiece showdown when two goals

BACK TO EARTH...Ntcham is about to be congratulated by his team-mate.

side the first twenty-five minutes from Callum McGregor d Oliver Ntcham sealed the sixth trophy in his two ceptional campaigns in charge at Parkhead.

However, he had a warning for Scottish football when he id: "We can do better."

The Hoops gaffer asserted: "We set out to win three phies, but I need to push them even harder next year. iere are improvements we can make. We'll go away, cover and come back with big motivation in the summer."

The Cup victory elevated Rodgers' team above Jock ein's Celtic side of 1970 and Walter Smith's Rangers outfit 1994, who both fell at the final hurdle as they attempted ccessive trebles.

"For us to be the first team to have done it is a real ivilege and a real special day," added Rodgers. "Through the different eras of the game up here, certain teams have minated and then it flipped – and in all that time it was ver achieved.

"It will probably take time to enjoy it. My feelings are ore with the supporters, the players, the staff, the board at brought me in a few years ago. I'm so happy for them.

"However, I will certainly need to push them even harder xt season, no doubt about that. They won't get too many ts on the back, that's for sure. This is our job.

"We're here to win. I think we can be better. We dropped o many points this year, especially at home. Everyone cognised that this year was going to be difficult on the back last season, but to still churn that out and have that spirit d to produce good performances when you need to is pressive.

"We can be nothing but inspired by the Celtic support d their commitment to us. Wherever we go, they're vays there. To give them a day like today gives me real tisfaction.

"There's not many days in your life when you wake with a chance of creating history. The players had a ance to create a memory that will last the rest of their es." ■

Scottish Cup Results

January 20, 2018:
Fourth Round:
CELTIC 5 Forrest, Sinclair, Ntcham, Boyata, Edouard
BRECHIN CITY 0

Gordon; Lustig, Ajer, Boyata (sub: Bitton), Tierney; Brown (sub: Kouassi), Ntcham; Forrest, McGregor; Sinclair (sub: Johnston); Edouard.

February 10: Fifth Round:
CELTIC 3 Forrest (3)
PARTICK THISTLE 2 Doolan, Sammon

De Vries; Lustig, Ajer, Simunovic, Tierney; Brown, Ntcham; Forrest (sub: Kouassi), Musonda (sub: McGregor), Sinclair (sub: Edouard); Dembele.

March 3: Quarter-Final:
CELTIC 3 Dembele (2, 1pen), Edouard
MORTON 0

De Vries; Ajer, Compper (sub: McGregor), Simunovic, Tierney; Brown, Ntcham; Forrest, Rogic (sub: Musonda), Sinclair (sub: Edouard); Dembele.

April 15: Semi-Final:
CELTIC 4 Rogic, McGregor, Dembele (pen), Ntcham (pen)
RANGERS 0

Gordon; Lustig, Ajer, Boyata, Tierney; Brown, Ntcham; Forrest (sub: Roberts), Rogic (sub: Sinclair), McGregor; Dembele (sub: Griffiths).

May 19: Final:
CELTIC 2 McGregor, Ntcham
MOTHERWELL 0

Gordon; Lustig, Boyata, Ajer (sub: Simunovic), Tierney; Brown, Ntcham; Forrest (sub: Sinclair), Rogic (sub: Armstrong), McGregor; Dembele.

Eighth Wonder

Title win gives Lennon 'heebie-jeebies'!

STOPPAGE-TIME SUPERSTAR...Odsonne Edouard hits the late winner and celebrates Neil Lennon's return to Celtic.

ON the day Celtic clinched their eighth successive title with a runaway 3-0 triumph over Aberdeen at Pittodrie on May 4, 2019, Neil Lennon's verdict on the champions was extremely insightful.

The Irishman, in charge of the team in his interim capacity for the ninth Premiership encounter, didn't waste any time indulging in today's fairly absurd soccer jargon where some observations border on the incomprehensible and the man in the stand is often left wondering if they were at the same game as the the so-called expert.

Lennon, however, cut to the chase as his players cavorted around the north east following yet another annexing of the coveted crown. In his second time around as manager of the club, the forty-seven-year-old former skipper summed up the latest victory thus: "They give me the heebie-jeebies at times".

Possibly not the most eloquent of tributes to an assortment of players who had conquered all before them fo the eighth consecutive year, but it was a point well made by the man who answered the club's SOS three months earlier when Brendan Rodgers abruptly ended his two-and-a-half-year reign with a sharp exit for Leicester City.

Lennon acknowledged he had "big shoes to fill" when he returned to the Parkhead dug-out on an interim basis. He had twenty-four hours to put an assembly of talent together for a crucial February 27 league confrontation with Hearts at Tynecastle where Scotland's dominant force urgently require a win to maintain their pole position in the top flight.

A dramatic stoppage-time winner from Odsonne Edouard, signed on a permanent basis for a club record £10million from French giants Paris Saint-Germain in the summer, piloted the Glasgow side to three points which kep them eight ahead of nearest challengers Rangers.

BACK TO PARADISE... Neil Lennon celebrates his return as Celtic manager following the 2-1 Scottish Cup Final win over Hearts. His reward for helping the club to win two trophies in three months was a full-time contract.

THE FINAL FAREWELL...Brendan Rodgers with his seventh – and last – silverware triumph after the 1-0 League Cup success against Aberdeen.

Scottish Premier League Table

P	Team	Pld	W	D	L	GF	GA	GD	Pts
1	**Celtic – Champions**	**38**	**27**	**6**	**5**	**77**	**20**	**57**	**87**
2	Rangers	38	23	9	6	82	27	55	78
3	Kilmarnock	38	19	10	9	50	31	19	67
4	Aberdeen	38	20	7	11	57	44	13	67
5	Hibernian	38	14	12	12	51	39	12	54
6	Hearts	38	15	6	17	42	50	-8	51
7	St Johnstone	38	15	7	16	38	48	-10	52
8	Motherwell	38	15	6	17	46	56	-10	51
9	Livingston	38	11	11	16	42	44	-2	44
10	Hamilton	38	9	6	23	28	75	-47	33
11	St Mirren	38	8	8	22	34	66	-32	32
12	Dundee	38	5	6	27	31	78	-47	21

League Cup Final

December 2, 2018:

CELTIC 1 Christie
ABERDEEN 0

Bain; Lustig, Boyata (sub: Simunovic), Benkovic, Tierney; McGregor, Rogic (sub: Brown); Forrest (sub: Ntcham), Sinclair; Edouard.

Scottish Cup Final

May 25, 2019: **CELTIC 2** Edouard (2, 1 pen)
HEARTS 1 Edwards

Bain; Lustig, Simunovic, Ajer, Hayes (sub: Bitton); Brown, Rogic (sub: Ntcham); Forrest, McGregor, Johnston (sub: Sinclair); Edouard.

ONE...Ryan Christie smashes in a superb effort in the 1-1 draw against Motherwell at Fir Park in December.

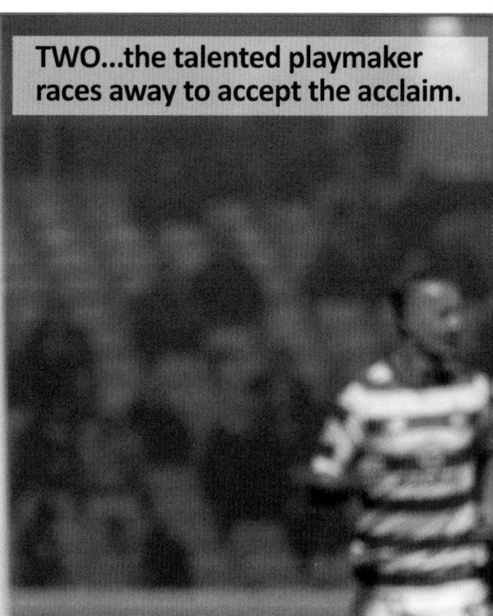

TWO...the talented playmaker races away to accept the acclaim.

THREE...Olivier Ntcham is the first to offer his congratulations to the grinning Christie.

FOUR...Christie is swamped by delighted team mates Scott Brown and Kieran Tierney with Filip Benkovic, Callum McGregor and Jonny Hayes about to join in.

WHAM...action man Kieran Tierney fires in an explosive long-range drive.

GRIM AND BEAR IT...Kiernan Tierney, Ryan Christie, Craig Gordon and Scott Sinclair look glum after a last-minute Motherwell equaliser.

TAKE-OFF FOR THE TITLE...Scott Brown leaps a hoarding after his late winner against Kilmarnock at Rugby Park in February.

Three days later, the new caretaker gaffer was back in Edinburgh with his players for the Scottish Cup quarter-final head-on collision with his former club Hibs at Easter Road. Many critics saw this as the match where the Hoops' hopes of an unprecedented treble treble could hit the rocks. Under Rodgers, Celtic went down meekly 2-0 on December 16 at the same venue to a team managed, fairly ironically, by Lennon.

Thin ice lay ahead in the capital, but the former Northern Ireland international midfielder worked wonders in galvanising the side who put in a thoroughly professional performance as they overcame the challenge of Hibs where two excellent second-half strikes from James Forrest, with a genuine contender for Goal of the Season, and skipper Scott Brown piloted them into the semi-final where they would meet Derek McInnes' Dons outfit.

It was back to points-gathering business the following week when the Pittodrie men were the visitors to the east end of Glasgow to grind out a goalless draw in a frustrating 90 minutes. It was not the second homecoming Lennon had planned, but he accepted a point on the road to the championship.

Another winning effort from Edouard was enough to cap a late, late show at Dens Park when he struck deep into added-on time consigning troubled Dundee to a loss on their way to the Premiership gallows.

All eyes were on Celtic Park on March 31 when Steven Gerrard brought his Ibrox squad across the Clyde for an intriguing meeting; Lennon's first against the club's ancient foes in seven years. Nitro met glycerine that pulsating afternoon as goals from Edouard, repaying every euro of his big-money transfer switch, and James Forrest gave the home side an important 2-1 victory.

The visitors were left with ten men in the first-half following controversial Colombian striker Alfredo Morelos' assault on Scott Brown when he fired his left elbow into the face of his opponent. Referee Bobby Madden had little option but to produce the red card, the Rangers player's fifth dismissal of the season.

Remarkably, Gerrard's team, despite their numerical disadvantage, produced a leveller though on-loan Liverpool winger Ryan Kent. The goal shook Celtic who were also left with ten men when Dedryck Boyata, in his last game for the club before his out-of-contract move to Bundesliga outfit Hertha Berlin, limped off with a ruptured hamstring.

With the clock ticking down, Edouard rolled a pass in front of the scampering Forrest and he didn't break stride as he carefully placed a measured close-range drive wide of the exposed Allan McGregor. In the immediate aftermath of the goal, Kent, inexplicably, lashed out at Brown and caught the Celt flush on the jaw.

The match officials missed the incident, but justice caught up with the Englishman through retrospective action from the Scottish Football Association when the misdeed was caught on camera. Deservedly, he copped a ban.

Poor old Broony was then subjected to a verbal tantrum from Rangers left-back Andy Halliday after the final whistle and that earned him a second yellow card and another suspension. On a day when emotions ran amok, Gerrard was also reported by the referee for comments, probably not too complimentary, and the Liverpool legend was invited to sit in the stand for the next match.

Celtic were well and truly in the driving seat and could even afford to lose at Ibrox on May 12 in an encounter

PYRAMID OF PLEASURE...Scott Brown leads the way with Ewan Henderson and Kristoffer Ajer following James Forrest's opening goal in Neil Lennon's comeback game in the 2-1 victory over Hearts at Tynecastle on February 27.

SCOTT SINCLAIR... flamboyant raider.

SCOTT BAIN... reliable keeper.

TOM ROGIC... the Wizard of Oz.

SCOTT BROWN... skipper supreme.

LEWIS MORGAN... ready for his big chance.

MIKEY JOHNSTON... the breakthrough Bhoy.

JEREMY TOLJAN...on loan fron Borussia Dortmund.

FILIP BENKOVIC...a year's deal from Leicester City.

JOZO SIMUNOVIC...assured central defender.

DEDRYK BOYATA... his four years at Celtic came to an end in the summer with a move to Hertha Berlin.

RYAN CHRISTIE... a revelation.

where only pride was at stake after Lennon had seen his side triumph at Pittodrie the previous week to make certain of another flag day at the Hoops.

They travelled to Aberdeen in the realisation they only required a solitary point to be crowned champions, but they accomplished the feat with a certain flourish and style with a three-goal trouncing of the north east outfit.

Mikael Lustig scored with a brilliant diving header just before the interval to send the Parkhead glory squad on their way to another massive celebration.

Jozo Simunovic nodded in a Callum McGregor corner-kick for the second while Odsonne Edouard rolled in the third in the fading moments.

Amazingly, it was Croatian central defender Simunovic's second goal in a week after scoring only two in his previous four years. The winner the previous week against Kilmarnock at a passion-loaded Parkhead came only five days after the death of club legend Billy McNeill at the age of 79. Both efforts were so reminiscent of the majestic McNeill with his aerial mastery and crucial goals during his glorious years at the club.

It was the visitors' sixth consecutive win at Pittodrie and they had now claimed seven goals at a tough venue in this campaign following their 4-3 victory on Boxing Day.

A happy, if slightly perplexed, Lennon said: "The players were fantastic today. They give me the heebie-jeebies sometimes with the way they play and take chances.

"We needed the opening goal because Aberdeen had had some great chances early on.

"I have to pay tribute to Brendan. He has to get a huge amount of credit. This title success is down to the foundations he laid here. I was lucky enough to carry it on.

"It's been really tough. It's been the toughest piece of management for me. I know from the outside people think it looks easy.

"But it's basically been coming in on your own and picking up. There was a lot of discontent around the club.

"It's a real privilege for me to be here as interim manager or as any manager."

Lennon has also paid tribute to his rock-solid rearguard who claimed another clean sheet during an impressive domestic campaign in 2019.

He added: "With all the emotions of what happened this week with Billy's funeral we had to keep calm. There was a lot of negativity around us and a lot of fake news.

"But the players have kept their focus really well.

"Scott Bain has been unbelievable since I came in. He made another world class save today.

"Simunovic and Ajer have formed a great partnership. Lustig has been a great player for this club for a long, long time and Tierney is a Celtic great already.

"It's a great moment for the players and the supporters."

On May 19, two goals from the precocious Mikey Johnston gave Celtic a 2-1 win over Hearts in a dress rehearsal for Hampden the following week. The crown was duly passed to Scott Brown and it was party time in Paradise yet again. ■

DANIEL ARZANI... hoping for better luck in his second loan season from Manchester City.

LEIGH GRIFFITHS... fans' favourite who had a troubled campaign.

JAMES FORREST... a key performer.

EWAN HENDERSON... a bright Bhoy.

OLIVIER NTCHAM...French midfield powerhouse.

OLIVER BURKE... a January loan signing from West Brom.

MIKAEL LUSTIG... dependable Swede.

CALLUM McGREGOR... big-time player.

TIMOTHY WEAH...returned early to Paris Saint-Germain.

SEASON 2018/2019

KIERAN TIERNEY... one of the Bhoys.

MOUSSA DEMBELE... season ended abruptly.

ODSONNE EDOUARD...the £10million man.

KRISTOFFER AJER...emerging central defender.

Premiership Results

August 4, 2018: **CELTIC 3** Rogic, Edouard, Ntcham (pen)
LIVINGSTON 1 Robinson
Gordon; Lustig, Ajer, Simunovic; Forrest, Brown, Ntcham, Hayes (sub: Tierney); Rogic (sub: Johnston), McGregor, Edouard (sub: Griffiths).

August 11: **HEARTS 1** Lafferty
CELTIC 0
Gordon; Lustig, Simunovic, Hendry, Tierney; Brown, Kouassi (sub: Rogic); Hayes (sub: Forrest), McGregor; Sinclair; Griffiths (sub: Edouard).

August 26: **CELTIC 1** Boyata
HAMILTON ACCIES 0
Gordon; Lustig, Boyata, Ajer; Brown, Rogic (sub: Ntcham); Forrest (sub: Johnston), McGregor, Tierney; Griffiths (sub: Christie); Dembele.

September 2 **CELTIC 1** Ntcham
RANGERS 0
Gordon; Lustig, Ajer, Boyata, Tierney; Brown, Ntcham; Forrest (sub: Sinclair), Rogic (sub: Christie), McGregor; Edouard (sub: Griffiths).

September 14: **ST MIRREN 0**
CELTIC 0
Gordon; Ajer, Boyata, Benkovic (sub: Griffiths), Tierney; Brown, Ntcham; Forrest, Rogic, McGregor, Edouard (sub: Christie).

September 23: **KILMARNOCK 2** Burke, Findlay
CELTIC 1 Griffiths
Gordon; Lustig, Boyata, Hendry, Tierney; Brown, Mulumbu (sub McGregor); Johnston (sub Edouard), Christie, Sinclair (sub: Morgan); Griffiths.

September 29: **CELTIC 1** Sinclair
ABERDEEN 0
Gordon; Lustig, Boyata, Hendry, Tierney; Brown, Ntcham (sub: Rogic); Forrest (sub: Morgan), McGregor, Edouard (sub: Sinclair); Griffiths.

October 7: **ST JOHNSTONE 0**
CELTIC 6 Forrest (4), Edouard, McGregor
Gordon; Lustig, Boyata, Benkovic (sub: Simunovic), Tierney; Forrest, Rogic (sub: Morgan), Ntcham, McGregor; Edouard, Griffiths (sub: Sinclair).

October 20: **CELTIC 4** Rogic, Ntcham, Edouard (2)
HIBS 2 Kamberi, McNulty
Gordon; Lustig, Boyata, Benkovic, Tierney; Brown (sub: Sinclair), Ntcham; Forrest (sub: Christie), Rogic (sub: Kouassi), McGregor; Edouard.

October 31: **DUNDEE 0**
CELTIC 5 Rogic, Sinclair (pen), Forrest, Edouard, Christie
Gordon; Lustig, Boyata (sub: Ajer), Benkovic, Tierney; Forrest, McGregor, Rogic (sub: Morgan), Christie, Sinclair; Edouard (sub: Arzani).

November 3: **CELTIC 5** Edouard (2), Benkovic, Forrest, Christie (pen)
HEARTS 0
Gordon; Lustig (sub: Ajer), Boyata, Benkovic, Tierney; McGregor, Christie, Rogic; Forrest, Sinclair (sub: Morgan); Edouard (sub: Johnston).

November 11: **LIVINGSTON 0**
CELTIC 0
Bain; Lustig, Boyata, Ajer (sub: Benkovic), Tierney; McGregor, Christie, Rogic; Forrest (sub: Morgan), Sinclair; Edouard.

November 24: **HAMILTON ACCIES 0**
CELTIC 3 Christie, Sinclair, Griffiths
Gordon; Lustig, Boyata, Benkovic, Tierney (sub: Izaguirre); Forrest (sub: Morgan), McGregor, Ntcham Christie; Edouard (sub: Griffiths), Sinclair.

December 5: **MOTHERWELL 1** Johnson
CELTIC 1 Christie
Gordon; Gamboa, Simunovic, Benkovic, Tierney; Brown, McGregor, Christie; Hayes (sub: Rogic), Ntcham (sub:Sinclair), Griffiths (sub: Edouard)

December 8: **CELTIC 5** Forrest (2), Edouard, Lustig, Christie
KILMARNOCK 1 Brophy (pen)
Gordon; Lustig, Simunovic, Benkovic, Izaguirre; McGregor, Rogic (sub: Ntcham); Forrest, Christie (sub: Brown), Sinclair; Edouard (sub: Griffiths).

December 16: **HIBS 2** Slivka, Kamberi
CELTIC 0
Gordon; Ajer, Simunovic, Benkovic, Izaguirre (sub: Hayes); Brown, Ntcham; Forrest, McGregor, Sinclair (sub: Morgan); Edouard (sub: Johnston).

December 19: **CELTIC 3** Ralston, Johnston (2)
MOTHERWELL 0
Gordon; Ralston, Simunovic, Benkovic, Izaguirre; Brown, Ntcham; Forrest, McGregor, Sinclair (sub: Morgan); Edouard (sub: Johnston).

December 22: **CELTIC 3** Johnston (2), Benkovic
DUNDEE 0
Bain; Ralston, Simunovic (sub: Ajer), Benkovic, Izaguirre; McGregor, Ntcham; Forrest (sub: Christie), Rogic, Sinclair; Johnston (sub: Hayes).

December 26: **ABERDEEN 3** May (pen), Cosgrove (pen), Ferguson
CELTIC 4 Sinclair (3), Edouard
Gordon; Lustig, Boyata, Benkovic, Izaguirre (sub: Hayes); Brown, McGregor (sub: Edouard), Rogic, Forrest (Sub: Ajer), Sinclair; Christie.

December 29: **RANGERS 1** Jack
CELTIC 0
Gordon; Lustig (sub: Ralston), Boyata, Benkovic (sub: Ajer), McGregor Brown, Ntcham, Christie; Forrest, Johnston (sub: Edouard), Sinclair.

anuary 23, 2019: **CELTIC 4** Burke (2), Sinclair (pen), Weah
ST MIRREN 0
ain; Lustig, Ajer, Benkovic, Izaguirre; Brown, McGregor; Forrest, hristie (sub: Henderson), Sinclair; Burke (sub: Weah).

anuary 26: **CELTIC 3** McGregor, Christie, Sinclair
HAMILTON ACCIES 0
ain; Lustig, Ajer, Benkovic, Izaguirre; Brown, McGregor; Johnston, hnston (sub: Forrest), Christie (sub; Bitton), Weah (Sub: Burke); nclair.

anuary 30: **CELTIC 2** McGregor, Christie
ST JOHNSTONE 0
ain; Lustig, Simunovic, Ajer, Izaguirre; Brown, McGregor; Forrest, hristie (sub: Bitton), Sinclair (sub: Weah); Burke (sub: Edouard).

ebruary 3: **ST JOHNSTONE 0**
CELTIC 2 Forrest, Weah
ain; Lustig (sub: Toljan), Ajer, Simunovic, Izaguirre; Brown, IcGregor; Forrest, Christie, Sinclair; Burke (sub: Edouard, ıb: Weah).

ebruary 6: **CELTIC 2** Christie, Burke
HIBS 0
ain; Toljan, Simunovic, Boyata (sub: Bitton), Izaguirre (sub: Hayes); rown, McGregor; Weah, Christie, Sinclair (sub: Johnston); Burke.

ebruary 17: **KILMARNOCK 0**
CELTIC 1 Brown
ain; Toljan, Boyata, Ajer, Hayes; Brown, McGregor; orrest (sub: Weah), Christie (sub: Bayo); Sinclair; douard (sub: Burke).

ebruary 24: **CELTIC 4** Sinclair, Edouard (2), Burke
MOTHERWELL 1 Ariyibi
ain; Toljan, Boyata, Ajer, Tierney (sub: Hayes); Bitton (sub: Burke), enderson; Forrest, Christie (sub: Hendry), Sinclair; Edouard.

ebruary 27: **HEARTS 1** Bozanic (pen)
CELTIC 2 Forrest, Edouard
ain; Toljan (sub: Lustig), Boyata, Ajer, Tierney; Brown, Bitton; Forrest, enderson (sub: Edouard), Sinclair (sub: Weah); Burke.

larch 9: **CELTIC 0**
ABERDEEN 0
ain; Toljan, Ajer, Boyata, Tierney; Brown, Bitton; Forrest, Henderson ub: Edouard), Sinclair (sub: Johnston); Burke (sub: Weah).

larch 17: **DUNDEE 0**
CELTIC 1 Edouard
ain; Toljan (sub: Weah), Lustig, Ajer (sub: Benkovic), Tierney; Brown, IcGregor; Forrest, Johnston (sub: Hayes), Sinclair; Edouard.

larch 31: **CELTIC 2** Edouard, Forrest
RANGERS 1 Kent
ain; Lustig, Boyata, Ajer Tierney (sub: Toljan); Brown, Ntcham ub: Rogic); Forrest, McGregor, Hayes (sub: Sinclair); Edouard.

April 3: **ST MIRREN 0**
CELTIC 2 Weah, Christie
Bain; Lustig (sub: Benkovic), Simunovic, Ajer, Izaguirre; Brown, Ntcham (sub: Christie), McGregor; Forrest, Weah (sub: Edouard), Burke.

April 6: **CELTIC 0**
LIVINGSTON 0
Bain; Simunovic, Benkovic (sub: Hayes), Ajer; Brown, McGregor, Rogic (sub: Weah), Christie (sub: Burke), Tierney; Forrest, Edouard.

April 21: **HIBS 0**
CELTIC 0
Bain; Lustig, Ajer, Simunovic, Izaguirre; Brown, Ntcham (sub: Rogic); Forrest (sub: Weah), McGregor, Hayes (sub: Sinclair); Edouard.

April 27: **CELTIC 1** Simunovic
KILMARNOCK 0
Bain: Lustig, Simunovic, Ajer, Izaguirre; Brown, Rogic (sub: Ntcham); Forrest (sub: Hayes), McGregor, Sinclair; Edouard.

May 4: **ABERDEEN 0**
CELTIC 3 Lustig, Simunovic, Edouard
Bain; Lustig (sub: Sinclair), Simunovic, Ajer, Tierney (sub: Hayes); Brown, Rogic; Forrest, McGregor, Weah (sub: Burke); Edouard.

May 12: **RANGERS 2** Tavernier, Arfield
CELTIC 0
Bain; Lustig (sub: Toljan), Simunovic, Ajer, Hayes; Brown, McGregor; Burke, Rogic (sub: Ntcham), Johnston (sub: Sinclair); Edouard.

May 19: **CELTIC 2** Johnston (2)
HEARTS 1 Mulraney
Bain; Ralston, Benkovic (sub: Simunovic), Ajer, Toljan; Bitton, Ntcham; Johnston, Henderson (sub: McGregor), Sinclair; Burke (sub: Dembele).

Good Christie!

Ryan is Hampden matchwinner

CELTIC 1
ABERDEEN 0
(December 2, 2018

HAIL THE CONQUERING HERO... Ryan Christie with the League Cup following his Hampden glory show.

RYAN CHRISTIE'S remarkable fairytale continued at Hampden on a grey and cold afternoon on December 2, 2018 when he scored the goal that won the League Cup against Aberdeen to give Brendan Rodgers his seventh successive domestic trophy since arriving in May 2016.

The midfielder had somersaulted from bit-part player in the Hoops' plans to become a key component.

And he emphasised that fact again against the Dons with a first-half stoppage-time goal that settled a tough, tense confrontation in front of a frenzied crowd at the national stadium.

Dedryck Boyata had just recovered from a sickening clas of heads with his ex-colleague Gary Mackay-Steven to send a clever long ball towards the enemy penalty area.

Christie timed his diagonal run to perfection as he got in behind the Dons rearguard with Shay Logan attempting to cover for his centre-backs.

The Highlander took an exquisite touch and fired a right-foot shot at goal that was blocked by the heroic Joe Lewis.

The rebound spun back to the Celt and this time he

THE WINNER...Ryan Christie slams the ball past Aberdeen keeper Joe Lewis for the only goal of the game.

CHEERS AND TEARS...Christie is about to be joined by Scott Sinclair as Lewis and Dons defender Shay Logan show their dejection.

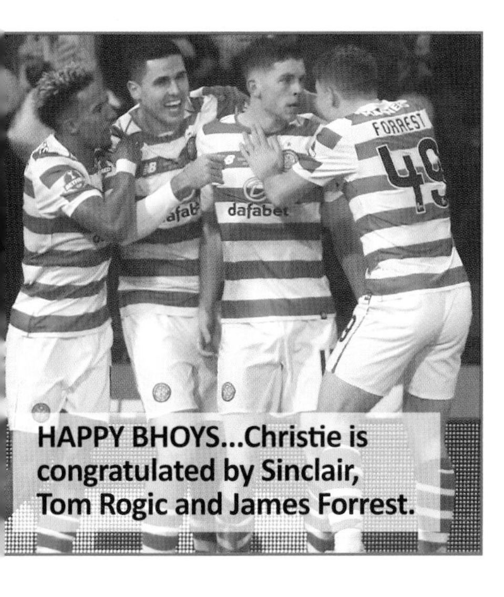

HAPPY BHOYS...Christie is congratulated by Sinclair, Tom Rogic and James Forrest.

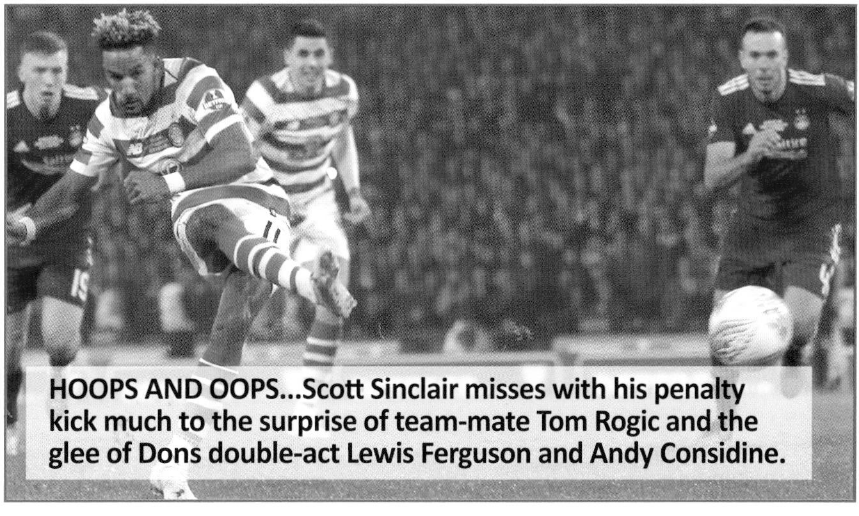

HOOPS AND OOPS...Scott Sinclair misses with his penalty kick much to the surprise of team-mate Tom Rogic and the glee of Dons double-act Lewis Ferguson and Andy Considine.

PARTY TIME...Scott Brown leads the celebrations after the victory over Aberdeen.

made no mistake with a venomous left-foot effort that kissed the underside of the crossbar on its way into the net.

At the end of a hectic, rollicking, frantic afternoon that turned out to be the goal that presented the trophy back to the holders – and signalled the astounding treble treble could now be on big-style.

Scott Sinclair squandered the opportunity to double the advantage eight minutes after the turnaround when he missed a penalty-kick.

To be absolutely fair, it didn't look a deliberate handball from Dom Ball and it also appeared to be a yard outside the area.

However, a spot-kick was awarded and possibly justice was done when Lewis plunged to his right to beat Sinclair's drive to safety.

Right from the first shrill of referee Andrew Dallas' whistle it was obvious the Dons were out to frustrate the Hoops.

Derek McInnes had devised a plan to man-mark his opponents with Ball never far away from Tom Rogic, Lewis Ferguson practically wearing the same shirt as Callum McGregor, Andrew Considine shadowed Odsonne Edouard everywhere while James Forrest and Sinclair had Max Lowe and Logan as constant companions.

Celtic were tasked with attempting to escape the shackles and it looked as though they had managed that feat in the seventh minute when Cup Final expert – and Dons' hoodoo man – Rogic had opened the way to triumph.

The Aussie midfielder accepted a pass from Forest, rolled it onto his left foot and from twenty-five yards fizzed a low drive away from the helpless Joe Lewis.

However the cries of "Goal!" from the Hoops contingent were silenced immediately when the ball thudded against the outside of the right-hand post and bounced harmlessly out of play.

Two minutes later, the Pittodrie outfit escaped again when a wayward kick from their keeper found Edouard. Unfortunately, the £10million French ace was sloppy with a pass to Forrest and the chance was lost.

In the sixteenth minute, Considine was rightly flagged offside when he thumped in a close-range drive following a left-wing corner-kick.

Scott Bain got down superbly to block the effort, but the standside match official had already spotted the infringement. However, credit the understudy keeper for lightning reflexes.

Amazingly, Forrest was the first player to be booked when Dallas decided he had attempted to stamp on the

FIRHILL FOR THRILLS...Moussa Dembele, in one of his last games for the Hoops in August, storms past a struggling Partick Thistle defender in the 3-1 second round win.

hallenging Lowe. The Dons left-back responded by pushing he winger in the back in a show of anger.

The Final was held up for almost ten minutes following he collision between Boyata and Mackay-Steven who both vent for a right-wing cross from Logan. The Belgian had to e helped off with blood on his shirt and he required some reatement on the touchline before returning with his head overed in bandages.

His former team-mate wasn't so fortunate and had to e stretchered off and taken immediately to hospital. 'hankfully, manager McInnes could confirm he was oncious and speaking at the end of the game.

Boyata limped off in the sixtieth minute to be replaced by ozo Simunovic and, incredibly, the Croatian almost netted n equaliser for the Dons with his first touch.

He swung wildly at a high cross into the box and the ransfixed Bain was helpless as the ball clattered off the unction of bar and post and, thankfully, bounced away.

Celtic, who also brought on Scott Brown and Olivier Ntcham for Rogic and Forrest to keep things tight nearing he end of the encounter, had their chances to kill off the ame.

Notably when Sinclair was sent through after a lung-ursting forty-yard run from McGregor saw him push a pass into the Englishman's tracks inside the box. However, underlining this was not to be his finest game in a hooped shirt, he carelessly lifted the ball over the crossbar.

Edouard, too, could have cemented the triumph in the fading moments when he dashed forward and had four team-mates screaming for a pass. However, the striker saw his name in lights and went for it himself.

His tame effort was blocked and Celtic had to withstand another counter-attack.

When the smoke of battle cleared, Brendan Rodgers had won his twenty-second domestic Cup-tie in his 150th game as Hoops manager.

Hampden goal hero Christie immediately thanked manager Rodgers for keeping faith in him.

The classy playmaker, who signed a new three-year deal at the champions the previous month, came into the first team as a second-half substitute against Hearts in the semi-final of the competition eight games before the Cup Final.

The 23-year-old helped turn the game around against the Edinburgh side and was involved in the three goals that saw the Parkhead men book their spot against the Dons.

Christie, who scored a sublime third goal at Murrayfield in October, had been a revelation ever since and was well worthy of his new contract with the champions. ▶

LEAGUE CUP CAMPAIGN

FINAL KISS-OFF...a bandaged Dedryck Boyata picks up his second last trophy as a Celtic player.

NUMBER ONE...Scott Bain enjoys his first Cup medal for Celtic.

IT TAKES TWO...boss Brendan Rodgers and skipper Scott Brown.

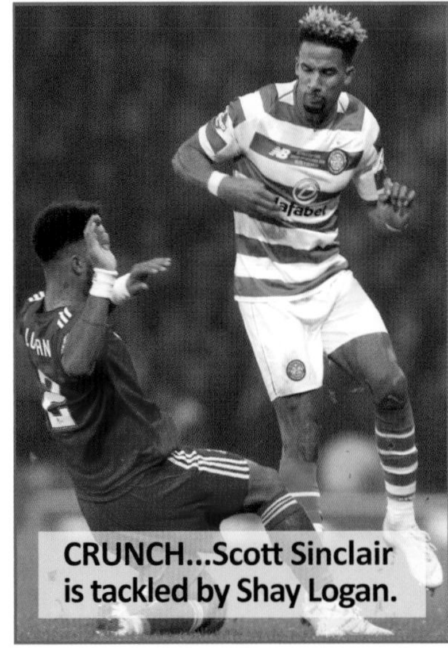

CRUNCH...Scott Sinclair is tackled by Shay Logan.

IN THE NICK OF TIME...Leigh Griffiths hammers in a quarter-final winner against St. Johnstone in September.

The player returned to Parkhead after eighteen months n loan at Pittodrie and realised it would be a make-or-break ampaign. He accepted the challenge and is reaping the ewards.

He admitted: "I was delighted when I found out I was laying. It would have been easy for the manager to go ack to players who have played so well for him over the ears.

"But credit to him, he kept the same team that have been n form for the last few weeks and, thankfully, it paid off.

"I had a lot of mixed emotions going into a big game, aving to play a lot of my old team-mates.

"Every single time we play them that's exactly what you et, they follow you all over the back, so to get over the line a close one, and obviously we had chances, is amazing.

"I'm just so so happy. Especially for all the boys who have orked with me and I think we deserved to win.

"I said when I signed the new deal I wanted to take ophies back so to get one so early in the season is pretty pecial."

Christie was asked about the chances of Celtic pulling off e remarkable feat of three domestic clean sweeps.

He answered: "We're not allowed to speak about that just et."

Rodgers wasn't quite so reticent, though, when he alked about the matchwinner. He admitted: "I am very atisfied. It was a very tough game for us on the back of tough week of fixtures, but the moment of real quality on us the game in terms of us keeping possession and en made the right moment to penetrate and it was a rilliant finish by Ryan.

"That's the way the football gods work. He'd been on oan at Aberdeen for eighteen months, which helped his evelopment and he comes back and you see the player, e's fantastic and he ends up getting the winning goal and Ian of the Match.

"He's shown that he has the personality to play at a big lub. He just needed time and I felt when I came in he wasn't eady to play every week.

"Rather than waste the talent, he needed to go out and lay every week, so he did that and he came back a stronger layer, more physical, with better knowledge of the game nd he's been absolutely brilliant for us."

Rodgers added: "The only disappointment for me is I felt e could have closed the game out sooner.

"We had the penalty and missed that, but we had about our breakaways. The situation at the end where it was four s one and we didn't make the right pass.

"The players are absolutely amazing, the heart they have, e fight when they're really tired and against a really physical eam like Aberdeen, they really test you so I am so proud of hem and so satisfied for them that they got another trophy.

"Very proud, but our notion is to keep looking forward. Great experience again for us on this ocasion. Great joy for he supporters and, like I say, we're very hungry to continue o win more.

"This was the first trophy we could win, we've won it and 'm very proud of the team."

Astonishingly, it was to be the last honour Brendan Rodgers would win as Celtic manager. ■

League Cup Results

August 18, 2018: Second Round:
PARTICK THISTLE 1 Mbuyi-Mutombo
CELTIC 3 Griffiths, Dembele, Rogic

Bain; Gamboa, Hendry, Ajer, Izaguirre; Brown, Ntcham (sub: McGregor); Johnston (sub: Forrest), Rogic, Sinclair; Griffiths (sub: Dembele).

September 26: Quarter-Final:
ST JOHNSTONE 0
CELTIC 1 Griffiths

Bain; Lustig, Boyata, Ajer (sub: Hendry), Tierney; Brown, Ntcham; Forrest, McGregor (sub: Rogic), Edouard; Griffiths.

October 28: Semi-Final:
HEARTS 0
CELTIC 3 Sinclair (pen), Forrest, Christie

Bain; Lustig, Ajer (sub: Hendry), Benkovic, Tierney; Kouassi (sub: Sinclair), Ntcham (sub: Christie); Forrest, Rogic, McGregor; Edouard.

December 2: Final:
CELTIC 1 Christie
ABERDEEN 0

Bain; Lustig, Boyata (sub: Simunovic), Benkovic, Tierney; McGregor, Rogic (sub: Brown); Forrest (sub: Ntcham), Sinclair; Edouard.

SHARING THE JOY...triumphant double-act James Forrest and Tom Rogic at Hampden.

Très Magnifique

French ace fires Celtic into history books

THE £10MILLION HISTORY BHOY... Odsonne Edouard celebrates the goal that brought the glorious treble treble.

CELTIC 2 HEARTS 1 (May 25, 2019)

ODSONNE EDOUARD had already made Celtic history as the club's most expensive player, so it was somehow appropriate the French star was the man who delivered even more to the club's extraordinary folklore in the 2-1 Scottish Cup Final triumph over Hearts at Hampden on May 25 2019.

With the team toiling and trailing 1-0 to a Ryan Edwards strike, it was the £10million frontman, signed on a permanent deal from Paris Saint-Germain in the summer, who stepped up to fire the club to a phenomenal treble treble.

Edouard took centre stage in the club's annals of fame when he strode onto a pass from Jonny Hayes in the sixty-first minute and had Christophe Berra chasing and Bobby Zlamal racing from his line to try to bail out his defence.

The talented striker weaved to his left as the keeper went down to make contact and referee Willie Collum had no hesitation in awarding a penalty-kick.

Edouard took a couple of steps back as the Celtic fans in the Hampden crowd held their collective breath before ambling forward in nonchalant fashion and thumping the ball low to the goalie's right hand and in at the post.

It was the lifeline a Hoops outfit required urgently on a day when they failed to spark. But they deserve the utmost credit for coming back so quickly and so positively after the loss of a dreadful goal in the fifty-third minute.

The defence failed to deal with a simple throw-in on the left when Arnauld Djoum lost James Forrest before the ball fell to Sean Clare who back-heeled it in front of the unmarked Edwards who found far too much space in the danger zone.

He could hardly believe the acres he was afforded as he rattled a shot through the legs of Scott Bain for a sensational opening goal. It was also a resounding wake-up call for a strangely lethargic and sloppy Celtic outfit.

The first-half passed with the Hoops failing to take control and lacking cohesion in their forward play which wasn't helped with some wayward distribution from keeper Bain.

He gifted the Edinburgh side a goal at Parkhead the

THAT WINNING SMILE... Callum McGregor holds the glittering prize.

SCOTTISH CUP CAMPAIGN

ONE...James Forrest fires an unstoppable drive high into the Aberdeen net for the semi-final breakthrough goal.

TWO...Odsonne Edouard fires home with a right-footed penalty-kick.

THREE...Tom Rogic sizzles in a left-foot clincher.

GLORY BHOY... Scott Brown celebrates even more silverware success at Hampden – his NINETEENTH medal as a Celt.

revious week and looked nervy with the ball at his feet n far too many occasions to make life comfortable for his eam-mates, the manager or the fans.

It wasn't all down to the keeper, of course, as Celtic ouldn't get into their rhythm or find any cohesion with their assing. Forrest and Mikey Johnston were starved of service, douard needed support and Scott Brown was spending far oo much time passing the ball sideways and backwards.

There was precious little on show in the opening 45 ninutes to excite the fans of the champions with their team n the brink of a phenomenal achievement.

In the sixth minute, there was a bright passage of play on he left when Johnston shimmied inside before rolling a pass) the overlapping Jonny Hayes, but his low cross was ooted for a corner at the near post by Christophe Berra.

Callum McGregor then picked up possession in midfield nd released Tom Rogic who touched the ball in front of douard, but John Souttar read the move and got across to lock the shot from the Frenchman.

And so it continued after the interval with Celtic showing bit more urgency and Hayes blowing a good opportunity as he team broke forward. The Irishman had a rush of blood to he head and elected to have a blast at goal from long range nd missed by miles while four team-mates didn't look too npressed as they swarmed into good positions.

But there was a praiseworthy response to losing a goal hat could have been prevented all along the line and douard's leveller from the spot was impressive with the youngster showing wonderful composure under so much pressure.

And he did it again in the eighty-second minute when Mikael Lustig headed a ball forward that fell perfectly for the aware striker with the Hearts defensive double-act of Berra and Souttar split for the only time in the game.

Edouard took the ball in his stride in an instant, raced forward, enticed Zlamal from his line and with the greatest of ease stroked the ball away from the keeper and into the inviting net.

Neil Lennon made changes as he strengthened the team as the clock ticked down towards history and Olivier Ntcham, Scott Sinclair and Nir Bitton came on for Rogic, Johnston and Hayes.

Five minutes were added on as nerve ends stretched to snapping point before the referee eventually blew for full-time.

The Celtic players stood at Hampden for that moment as it dawned on them what they had achieved.

Lennon was clearly emotional as he fell to his knees on the touchline.

Memories are made of this.

Only moments afterwarwards the club confirmed they had offered Lennon the manager's job on a permanent basis and, still covered in champagne, the Irishman was already plotting the way ahead as he acknowledged there would have to be a squad rebuild.

He said: "There's a good core there, lots on long-term ▶

THE BANNER SAYS IT ALL...the Celtic fans lap up their club's moment of history.

CELEBRATIONS... James Forrest displays his delight at the full-time whistle.

contracts that's great. There will be personnel leaving and coming in.

"It may be a short holiday, there's a process in work at the minute that we've identified some players. Hopefully, we can get some freshness and quality in the squad as soon as possible.

"You could see against Hearts, they are cramping and tugging at muscle injuries. It is a monumental effort to do what they've done over three years. I don't know how many games they have played domestically and in Europe.

"I'd like us to be a bit more on the front foot attacking-wise, not maybe use the goalkeeper as much. I know we use the sweeper keeper a lot these days, but build the team around my centre-forwards, as well.

"Odsonne Edouard has carried the flame brilliantly and did it again on this occasion, we've had one fit centre-forward in the building since I've come in and he's taken on that responsibility magnificently and this was another big show from him in a big game. He's put himself in the annals of the club's history.

"I like him a lot, his temperament and his quality is fantastic."

Skipper Scott Brown was swift to add his contribution to the managerial announcement by insisting Lennon was the right man to lead Celtic to nine in a row and beyond.

The 33-year-old inspirational midfielder, who lifted his NINETEENTH Hoops honour at the national stadium following the latest victory, revealed the reaction from his team-mates when they heard the news.

Brown said: "We all found out on Twitter and all the lads are diving about in the changing room. We went out, got the gaffer and brought him back in. The cheer for the manager to get the job – it was phenomenal. He deserves it. It has been a hard one since he came in, but he's the only man in my eyes for the job.

"He has had to win two trophies and yet again he has

ıown that he knows how to win trophies. He's a fantastic ıan manager and he's been fantastic since he came in. .e speaks well and every single one in that changing room ıves him.

"I don't think there is a better person for the job. The ressure this job brings on everyone, for us to do eight in row, for him to push us towards, hopefully, nine, for me ıows he's the right man for the job for the club.

"It's a great appointment at a great time. We need to push ı next season. The Champions League is the big one at the art, we need to make sure we continue the form as we have een.

"The recruitment of players is going to be a thing, ıere will be a change in the team because of what Brendan odgers had and what Neil is going to go out and do. ın sure it will be a breeze.

WONDER BHOY...sixteen-year-old Karamoko Dembele enjoys his Hampden experience.

Scottish Cup Results

January 19, 2019:
Fourth Round:
CELTIC 3 Sinclair (2), Weah
AIRDRIE 0
Bain; Ralston, Boyata, Benkovic, Izaguirre; Brown (sub: Bitton), McGregor; Forrest (sub: Johnston), Christie, Sinclair (sub: Weah); Burke.

February 9:
Fifth Round:
CELTIC 5 Sinclair (3), Brown, Forrest
ST JOHNSTONE 0
Bain; Toljan, Boyata, Simunovic (sub: Ajer), Hayes; Brown, McGregor; Forrest, Christie (sub: Edouard), Sinclair; Burke (sub: Weah).

March 2:
Quarter-Final:
HIBS 0
CELTIC 2 Forrest, Brown
Bain; Lustig, Boyata (sub: Toljan), Ajer, Tierney; Brown, Bitton; Forrest, Edouard, Sinclair (sub: Johnston); Burke (sub: Henderson).

April 14:
Semi-Final:
CELTIC 3 Forrest, Edouard (pen), Rogic
ABERDEEN 0
Bain; Lustig, Simunovic, Ajer, Tierney; Brown, McGregor; Forrest (sub: Weah), Christie (sub: Rogic), Hayes (sub: Sinclair); Edouard.

May 25:
Final:
CELTIC 2 Edouard (2, 1 pen)
HEARTS 1 Edwards
Bain; Lustig, Simunovic, Ajer, Hayes (sub: Bitton); Brown, Rogic (sub: Ntcham); Forrest, McGregor, Johnston (sub: Sinclair); Edouard.

"He has won us the league and won a semi-final and a Cup Final. That shows the kind of man he is.

"He could have distanced himself from the job because of what Brendan did. But when he got called, he answered that call."

The calmest player on a tension-laden afternoon with so much at stake was Odsonne Edouard who actually looked suprised when the TV interviewer asked him if he was on edge before he took the crucial penalty-kick against the Edinburgh side.

The 21-year-old flamboyant forward smiled and replied: "I am never nervous. So, when I took the penalty I believed I would score. I was confident.

"I'm very happy. It's special because it's the treble treble. And I'm very happy for this."

The impressive youngster added: "I have just been told about the manager and it's good news. This is a good achievement for the players and I'm very happy to work with the coach."

Neil Lennon and Odsonne Edouard could be a double-act made in Paradise. ■

Singing in the Reign

PYRAMID OF PLEASURE...Lou Macari, Harry Hood and Jimmy Johnstone celebrate a goal.

Jinky Wonder Show wins title at Ibrox

CELTIC had the opportunity to clinch a memorable league and Cup double on the evening of Wednesday May 3, 1967 at Parkhead, only four days after Willie Wallace had netted both goals in the showpiece showdown with Aberdeen at Hampden.

The newly-won Scottish Cup was paraded in front of 44,000 fans, a following who fully expected to see their favourites crowned Scottish First Division champions for the second successive season. Dundee United, the only Scottish team to have beaten them back on Hogmanay, were the opposition.

To underline the achievement of Jock Stein's team requiring a solitary point to clinch the crown, you only have to look at the condition of Scottish football as a whole at the time. Despite their extraordinary Scottish Cup defeat at Berwick in January, Rangers had quickly stabilised and had actually won through to the European Cup-Winners' Cup Final where they would meet and lose 1-0 to Bayern Munich in Nuremberg a week after Celtic were due to play in the European Cup Final in Lisbon.

Adding weight to the strength and competitiveness of the top flight was the accomplishment of Kilmarnock in reaching the UEFA Cup semi-final where they lost 4-2 on aggregate to a Dinamo Zagreb side which went on to beat Leeds United 2-0 in the two-legged Final. The Slavs had knocked out Dunfermline earlier on the away goals rule after the tie had finished level at 4-4. In the same tournament, Dundee United humbled the mighty Barcelona 4-1 on aggregate, winning home and away, before losing 3-1 to Juventus.

It took an exceptional manager with a special set of footballers to impose their superiority. Step forward, Jock Stein and his Celtic players.

However, their Tannadice opponents in Glasgow that evening were clearly not there to just make up the numbers. Playing an offensive team such as Celtic fitted seamlessly into their counter attacking strategy. And they proved it for the second time in that campaign; Celtic suffering once more as they fell for soccer's classic sucker-punch in an uncharacteristic anti-climax.

They had gone into the game in the realisation they had not lost a league game at home since April 17, 1965 when they went down 2-1 to Partick Thistle, although it would be fair to assume the players on that particular Saturday might have been concentrating on the Scottish Cup Final against Dunfermline the following week.

Everything looked to be going according to plan when Celtic were awarded a penalty-kick in the twenty-fifth

SEASON 1966/1967

League Table Top Ten

P	Team	Pld	W	D	L	GF	GA	GD	Pts
1	**Celtic**	**34**	**26**	**6**	**2**	**111**	**33**	**78**	**58**
2	Rangers	34	24	7	3	92	31	61	55
3	Clyde	34	20	6	8	64	48	16	46
4	Aberdeen	34	17	8	9	72	38	34	42
5	Hibernian	34	19	4	11	72	49	23	42
6	Dundee	34	16	9	9	74	51	23	41
7	Kilmarnock	34	16	8	10	59	46	13	40
8	Dunfermline Athletic	34	14	10	10	72	52	20	38
9	Dundee United	34	14	9	11	68	62	6	37
10	Motherwell	34	10	11	13	59	60	−1	31

League Cup Final

October 29, 1966: **CELTIC 1** Lennox
RANGERS 0

Simpson; Gemmell, O'Neill; Murdoch, McNeill, Clark; Johnstone, Lennox, McBride, Auld, Hughes (sub: Chalmers).

Scottish Cup Final

April 29, 1967: **CELTIC 2** Wallace (2)
ABERDEEN 0

Simpson; Craig, Gemmell; Murdoch, McNeill, Clark; Johnstone, Wallace, Chalmers, Auld, Lennox.

European Cup Final

May 25, 1967: **CELTIC 2** Gemmell, Chalmers
INTER MILAN 1 Mazzola (pen)

Simpson; Craig, Gemmell; Murdoch, McNeill, Clark; Johnstone, Wallace, Chalmers, Auld, Lennox.

THE CUP THAT CHEERS...Jock Stein proudly holds the European Cup, the pinnacle of his considerable managerial achievements. Celtic became the first British team to conquer Europe when they memorably overcame Inter Milan 2-1 in Lisbon on May 25, 1967.

LORD OF THE WING...Jimmy Johnstone could terrorise any defence.

minute after Bobby Lennox had been sent tumbling in the box. Tommy Gemmell fairly thrashed his effort wide of goalie Sandy Davie. It remained that way with the champions-elect strangely failing to ignite, despite the desperate and vocal exhortations from the terracings.

The Tannadice men kept their powder dry until the fifty-fourth minute when, unusually, Billy McNeill and John Clark went walkabout and Billy Hainey got in behind the central defenders, drew Ronnie Simpson from his line, rounded the exposed keeper and stroked the ball unerringly into the vacant net. A hush greeted the goal.

However, the fans found their collective voice seven minutes later when Willie Wallace restored Celtic's advantage. Centre-half Doug Smith and keeper Davie made a terrible mess of attempting to deal with a hanging cross into the box and the ever-alert Wallace seized on the loose ball to roll it home with ease. That was the signal for mass celebrating among the fans, but, astonishingly, United came back again to equalise.

In the sixty-eighth minute, the home defence didn't deal with a routine corner-kick and Dennis Gillespie, who had scored at Tannadice in December, was allowed to run in uninterrupted to send a header flying past Simpson.

Once more, an unanticipated cloud of trepidation materialised over the ground. The supporters knew, though, that a point would still be good enough to win the title. Three minutes after Gillespie's effort, Jackie Graham sneaked through to snatch a third for a United side who were refusing to follow the script. Celtic lost 3-2 for the second time to the same opponents and still required a point to make sure the flag would be flying over Parkhead at the start of the new season.

Tommy Gemmell had an interesting spin on the situation. "Ach, we weren't too bothered. We knew the next game was against Rangers on the Saturday and we fancied winning the title at Ibrox."

Inter Milan supremo Helenio Herrera, immaculately-coiffured and expensively-dressed, took his front row seat at storm-lashed Ibrox Stadium on Saturday May 6 as Celtic set out to make history by lifting the championship at the ground of their greatest rivals.

The bloated grey skies over Glasgow had burst from early morning and the torrential rain poured down vigorously, practically in rivulets, creating havoc with the electrics throughout the city and bringing the underground to a virtual standstill. Even the attendance was shy of the 90,000 anticipated with 78,000 fans in the stadium in time for kick-off. Various travel services had been severely curtailed during the freakish monsoon conditions.

The Ibrox playing surface very swiftly resembled a quagmire. However, the underfoot swamp failed to prevent the players from both teams from serving up breathtaking entertainment with little Jimmy Johnstone taking top billing in a fascinating 2-2 draw where Celtic were a mere nine minutes away from their first league win in Govan in nine years.

Adventurous left-back Gemmell recalled: "Jinky was immense that day. What made the achievement even more remarkable was the fact the entire game was played in a downpour. He should have disappeared in the mud, but he decided to turn it on. His shirt was drenched and sodden and falling off his shoulders, his boots were just about submerged in the glaur, but nothing was going to deter him taking centre stage. Up against him that afternoon was Davie Provan, who was a tall, rangy guy.

"If Helenio Herrera had arrived in Glasgow believing Jimmy Johnstone was merely a run-of-the-mill outside-right then he got on his Milan-bound flight with different ideas. Jinky capped a wonderful display – easily one of the best I have ever seen by an individual player anywhere – with a soaring left-foot shot into the roof of the net from about twenty-five yards. Norrie Martin was in the Rangers goal that afternoon and he took off in determined fashion, but there was no way he was going to prevent that effort from rattling the rigging."

WELL DONE, MY SON...Jock Stein and Billy McNeill, his skipper, always had a special bond – as it clearly shows in this image after yet another win.

After his usual careful deliberation before any game, but articularly against Rangers, Jock Stein fielded the team he vould choose to represent Celtic in the dramatically-changed ircumstances of Lisbon later that month. He was resolute in is determination to clinch the club's second successive hampionship at Ibrox.

Bertie Auld insisted: "Publicly, Big Jock would inform veryone that a meeting with Rangers was just another game. rivately, the players all knew just how much he enjoyed utting one over our old rivals. I would go as far as to say he etested Rangers. I don't think that is too strong a word. He eally disliked them."

So, the Celtic manager would have been far removed from est pleased when Rangers scored their first goal against eltic that season after their 4-0 trouncing in the Glasgow up, the 2-0 loss in the league at Parkhead and the 1-0 defeat 1 the League Cup Final at Hampden. There was little Ronnie impson could do as Sandy Jardine's ferocious right-foot venty-yarder crashed into the net.

The Ibrox players must have thought the strike had resented them with a half-time lead as it arrived in the rty-first minute. However, Celtic, displaying the qualities xpected of genuine champions, equalised within sixty econds. Bobby Lennox squeezed a low drive away from the prawling Norrie Martin and then groaned in dismay as the all collided with the far post. His disappointment dissipated 1 a heartbeat as Johnstone, lurking with intent and reacting nore swiftly than the Rangers defence, plonked the rebound nto the net.

In the seventy-fourth minute, Celtic's miniature sorcerer onjured up an inspirational virtuoso moment that was nmediately seared into the memory banks of anyone rtunate enough to witness his generous gift of the extraordinary. The slight winger, after gliding on to a right-wing throw-in from Stevie Chalmers, somehow dredged himself across the soaking marsh with Rangers defender Davie Provan quite content to pass him inside onto his 'weaker' left foot.

From somewhere within that slight frame, Johnstone found the reserves of strength to take a touch and then heave an utterly unstoppable shell high past Martin into the keeper's top right-hand corner of his net. He was immediately submerged by his delighted team-mates as the home defenders argued among themselves.

They had just been in the presence of genius and had no need to attempt to apportion blame. Johnstone, swinging his arms like a happy schoolboy, trotted over to his outside-right berth as Rangers prepared to recentre the ball.

With time running out, Willie Henderson cut inside to drill a low shot across Simpson towards the far corner. The mud-spattered custodian got down to it in a flash, but, unhappily though, he couldn't keep hold of the greasy ball and it squirmed loose into the tracks of Roger Hynd, a muscle-bound wing-half converted to centre-forward for this game, and he couldn't fail to miss from four yards.

Nine minutes later, referee Willie Syme, a match official who would never receive a Christmas card from Jock Stein, blew for time-up. Sportingly, John Greig, the despondent Rangers captain, was the first to congratulate Johnstone with Provan next in line. At least, they realised they had faced an irresistible force that damp day in Govan.

Earlier in the historic campaign, a strike from Bobby Lennox was enough to give Celtic the League Cup against the Ibrox side in a tense October 29 encounter at Hampden.

It was the start of something good. ■

Double Delight

Celtic's historic day in the sun

HAMPDEN PARK was bathed in glorious sunshine on the day Bobby Lennox sizzled in an extraordinary hat-trick as Celtic overwhelmed Hibs 6-2 in the League Cup Final on April 5, 1969.

It was a historic occasion when smart observers claimed Jock Stein's conquering heroes actually won TWO trophies on the same afternoon.

As Buzzbomb Bobby and his team-mates decimated the Easter Road men, a result emerged elsewhere that virtually handed the Parkhead side their fourth successive First Division championship to sit nicely with their fourth League Cup on the spin. Nearest challengers Rangers collapsed to a 2-1 upset against Dundee United at Tannadice and, while it's true the Ibrox side's loss went a long way to guaranteeing Celtic the crown yet again, the title was not finally settled until the 2-2 draw with Kilmarnock at Rugby Park on April 21.

Two league games later after the dust had settled on another exhilarating campaign, Jock Stein's side sat comfortably in pole position with fifty-four points from thirty-four games, five more than their Ibrox rivals.

The only thing on the Celtic manager's mind on an April afternoon at the national stadium, though, was the League Cup confrontation against an Edinburgh team that had eked out a 1-1 draw in Glasgow the previous month. Hibs were the chameleons of Scottish football. One week, wonderful; the next, woeful. They would complete the league season in joint twelfth place alongside Clyde. Remarkably, considering their playing resources, they lost fifteen games.

REST AND NO PLAY...for the time being! A rare image of Bobby Lennox taking it easy on the beach at Saltcoats.

And yet they could point to quality players among their ranks such as reliable goalkeeper Thomson Allan, who would go to the 1974 World Cup Finals as the Scotland back-up to David Harvey, Pat Stanton, who would enjoy an Indian Summer at Parkhead, John Blackley, an international defender, astute midfielder Peter Cormack, who would go onto play for Liverpool, and snake-hipped winger Peter Marinello, who, only nine months later, joined Arsenal for £100,000, a phenomenal amount for a Scottish player at the time.

For twenty-three minutes they kept an eager Celtic side at bay. Inside an hour, though, they had conceded six goals and were in football's equivalent of hell. Willie Wallace drew first blood when Bertie Auld, with his usual precision, curled a free-kick into the penalty area. Stanton managed to head clear, but the ball dropped straight at the feet of Wallace who rattled it through a ruck of players and beyond the reach of Allan.

Auld was enjoying the occasion as he strutted around the immaculate playing surface, spraying passes hither and yon as he probed for weaknesses in his opponents' defence. Not content with exploiting the gaps for his team-mates, the masterful Auld decided to add his name to the scoresheet. On the half-hour mark, he released Stevie Chalmers who scurried down the left before pitching over a teasing cross. Auld struck it first time with his left foot and the next time Allan saw the ball was when he was fishing it from the back of his net.

The Hibs players were looking forward to the sanctuary

SEASON 1968/1969

League Table Top Ten

P	Team	Pld	W	D	L	GF	GA	GD	Pts
1	**Celtic**	**34**	**23**	**8**	**3**	**89**	**32**	**57**	**54**
2	Rangers	34	21	7	6	81	32	49	49
3	Dunfermline Athletic	34	19	7	8	63	45	18	45
4	Kilmarnock	34	15	14	5	50	32	18	44
5	Dundee United	34	17	9	8	61	49	12	43
6	St Johnstone	34	16	5	13	66	59	7	37
7	Airdrieonians	34	13	11	10	46	44	2	37
8	Heart of Midlothian	34	14	8	12	52	54	−2	36
9	Dundee	34	10	12	12	47	48	−1	32
10	Morton	34	12	8	14	58	68	−10	32

League Cup Final

April 5, 1969: **CELTIC 6** Wallace, Auld, Lennox (3), Craig
HIBS 2 O'Rourke, Stevenson

Fallon; Craig, Gemmell (sub: Clark); Murdoch, McNeill, Brogan; Johnstone, Wallace, Chalmers, Auld, Lennox.

Scottish Cup Final

April 26, 1969: **CELTIC 4** McNeill, Lennox, Connelly, Chalmers
RANGERS 0

Fallon; Craig, Gemmell; Murdoch, McNeill, Brogan; Connelly, Wallace, Chalmers, Auld, Lennox.

BHOYS ZONE

WILLIE WALLACE was the only player to be bought by Jock Stein for the legendary Lisbon Lions team that won the European Cup, beating Inter Milan 2-1 in the Portuguese capital on May 25, 1967.

The iconic Celtic manager splashed £30,000 to bring the versatile Scotland international forward from Hearts in December 1966.

Wallace went some way to repaying Stein's faith by scoring two goals in the 3-1 win over Dukla Prague in the semi-final.

CHEERS...Jock Stein acknowledges the applause from the Celtic fans, something the manager got used to over the years.

NET PROFIT...Jimmy Johnstone could make and take goals as he demonstrates with a close-range effort against Morton keeper Andy Crawford with defender Hugh Strachan vainly appealing for offside.

of their dressing room at half-time when lightning-swift Lennox struck for the third goal. Nothing could have been simpler. Jimmy Johnstone zipped in a right-wing corner-kick to the near-post and Lennox bolted in ahead of the massed ranks to get the merest of touches with his head to glide the ball away from an astonished Allan. Was there any point in restarting the game for the second period? Hibs, as everyone in the 74,240 crowd would surely have agreed, were a beaten team.

Thirteen minutes after the turnaround, Auld split the Edinburgh side's back lot and Lennox – "I'm convinced he was born fast," Danny McGrain was fond of saying – waltzed onto the pass, leaving gasping defenders in his slipstream, and drew Allan from his line before stroking the ball into the vacant net. If it had been a boxing match, the referee would have put the Edinburgh players out of their misery. No such luck in this particular sport, however. Celtic continued the trek towards Allan, who must have wondered about the wisdom of becoming a netminder.

Lennox completed his trio in the seventy-third minute and Jim Craig, who scored goals with the regularity of a sighting of Hally's Comet, slotted in the sixth from a tight angle. Jock Stein decided to give John Clark some exercise and sent him on for Tommy Gemmell. The defender's arrival coincided with two late goals from Hibs, Jimmy O'Rourke netting in the eighty-second minute and Eric Stevenson five minutes later. Apparently, Clark didn't even blush as he picked up his winner's medal.

The game had been due to take place in October, but had to be delayed because of a fire in the Hampden stand. Three weeks later, Celtic would return to the national stadium to take on Rangers in the Scottish Cup Final. Could they again manage a four-goal winning margin?

The answer was provided in another confrontation that was as good as over after the opening half. George Connelly had just turned twenty years of age the previous month and was a relatively unknown quantity among the Celtic first team squad,

However, after his supreme appearance in the Scottish Cup Final against the Ibrox foes, the Fifer was the player most acclaimed by the delighted followers of the newly-crowned treble winners. Connelly, though, should have been nowhere near the Parkhead first team that eventful afternoon when Jock Stein's all-conquering line-up completed their second silverware clean sweep in three years.

A suspension to Jimmy Johnstone opened the door for the precocious youngster as the Celtic manager revamped his tactics against a team that had hammered Aberdeen 6-1 in the semi-final at Parkhead while the Hoops beat Morton 4-1 at the national stadium, both games being played on the same afternoon.

The bookies made the Ibrox outfit favourites. Certainly, history was on Rangers' side – they had yet to be defeated in a Scottish Cup Final for forty years. Their Parkhead opponents hadn't beaten them in the competition's ultimate showdown since 1904.

Celtic would also be forced to line up without their balletic battering-ram John Hughes on the left wing. The twinkle-toed powerhouse had been getting twice-daily treatments on a leg injury during the week leading up to the grand finale, but had failed a late fitness test. Harry Hood, a clever, ball-playing forward bought from Clyde for a club record £40,000 the previous month, was unavailable as he was Cup-tied following a previous appearance in the competition for the Shawfield outfit.

Stein, on the face of it, looked to have team selection problems. Rangers, too, would be without £100,000 striker Colin Stein, whose rumbustious, up-and-at-'em approach to the beautiful game had brought a red card too many and his

FLASH HARRY...Jock Stein brought in Harry Hood from Clyde during the season and he was a shrewd acquisition. Here he nets against Morton keeper Erik Sorensen with defenders John Lavelle and Davie Hayes helpless.

'eward' would be a seat in the stand that afternoon. Alex 'erguson led the line against Celtic; he wasn't to know it, ut it would be his last outing for the club.

It was hardly a secret that Jock Stein enjoyed deploying vingers in his team and Jimmy Johnstone, on the right, and ohn Hughes, on the opposite flank, had been potent threats hat particular season. Now, though, he had to plan for a rucial confrontation without their services. Davie White, he youthful Rangers manager at a mere thirty-five, was eady to pit his tactical wits against his dug-out opponent. Ie lost big-style.

Stein created a Celtic eleven that would largely ignore aids on the flanks, although, of course, full-backs Jim Craig nd Tommy Gemmell would be encouraged to join the attack 'henever possible. Connelly was given the No.7 shorts and ertie Auld, who had kicked off his career as an outside-left, ppeared to have been given the opportunity to reprise the ole. White, apparently, accepted the dangling carrot.

Neither Connelly nor Auld played as wide Bhoys in the ame. Stein manoeuvred the pair into withdrawn midfield oles which flummoxed the Ibrox full-back pairing of Kai ohansen and Willie Mathieson. Without direct opponents deal with, the defensive duo were enticed further up the eld and Stevie Chalmers and Bobby Lennox, two forwards ifted with searing pace, were ordered to expose the space ehind Johansen and Mathieson. It was half-time before the onfused White could attempt to sort out the mayhem in his efence.

By then, it was a tad too late – Celtic were leading by ree clear goals and were well on their way to picking up e silverware.

Stein couldn't have wished for a more enterprising start. corner-kick was claimed on the left-wing and Lennox otted over to take it, as he had done so many times in the ast. His curling delivery eliminated the Ibrox players at the near post and skipper Billy McNeill was generously allowed a clear run at the ball. Majestically, he leapt and, straining his neck muscles to the limit, snapped his head forward, made perfect contact with the sphere and guided a header into keeper Norrie Martin's right-hand corner.

With the Rangers back lot still attempting vainly to unravel the conundrum that was presented before them, Celtic took full advantage by scoring two quickfire goals before the half-time whistle. George Connelly was a key player in both strikes. A minute from the interval, he intercepted a ball from Swedish winger Orjan Persson intended for Mathieson. With praiseworthy speed of thought, the youngster diverted a pass to Lennox who enjoyed the freedom of Hampden as he sped through before burying the ball behind the exposed Martin.

Precisely seventy-seven seconds later, Celtic eased to an unassailable three-goal advantage and it was the elegant Connelly who delivered the coup de grace. Martin, possibly still reeling at the loss of the Lennox goal, attempted a short goal-kick to his skipper John Greig, who clearly wasn't expecting the pass. As he tried to bring the ball under control, Connelly sauntered in, took it from him, sidestepped the goalkeeper and rolled a lazy effort into the net. The Celtic end in the 132,870 attendance erupted in joyous bedlam.

It was all over long before Stevie Chalmers, fourteen minutes from time, was invited to utilise the wide, open spaces of the playing field as he ran in unopposed before lobbing the ball over the right shoulder of the transfixed Martin.

Bertie Auld exclaimed afterwards: "I saw that performance from us twice; once today on the Hampden pitch and once on the manager's tactics board yesterday." Mischievously, he added: "You could say everything went according to plan." ■

Swede Dreams

Fifty-goal Larsson takes top billing

DREADLOCK HAPPY BHOY...Henrik Larsson in typical pose after a Celtic goal against old foes Rangers.

WITH his customary grace, Henrik Larsson eased onto the slide-rule pass from Jackie McNamara, drifted behind the unsuspecting Fernando Ricksen, lured Stefan Klos from his goal-line, pirouetted around the keeper and deftly stroked a left-foot shot into the net from the tightest of angles.

This consistent creator of fantasies, with a smile to match the occasion, held up both hands to the adoring supporters creating a din of delight in the Broomloan Road stand; the five fingers were extended on the right hand and the tips of the forefinger and the thumb on the left touched in a circle and, put together, they signified the number 50.

The Swede had just rolled in Celtic's third goal in a formidable 3-0 triumph over Rangers at Ibrox and, incredibly, the lithe and cultured attacker had just claimed his fiftieth strike of a memorable campaign, a sensational feat which would see him honoured with the coveted Golden Shoe award, the prize for European football's top goalscorer.

The date was April 29, 2001, it was Celtic's fourth triumph over Dick Advocaat's side – including a League Cup semi-final success – in five meetings and the title had already been won three weeks earlier when Tommy Johnson claimed the only goal of the game against St Mirren in front of the season's best attendance of 60,440 at a Celtic Park awash with euphoria.

The Premier League championship was duly delivered in style with the total points tally of ninety-seven setting a new record, seven better than the previous best.

Martin O'Neill's side already had the League Cup in the trophy cabinet following Larsson's hat-trick in the 3-0 success over Kilmarnock at Hampden on March 18. After the win over St Mirren, Celtic were one step removed from their first domestic treble since the heady days of the legendary Jock Stein in 1969.

Hibs barred their way to the milestone, the Edinburgh side lying in wait after reaching the Scottish Cup Final which would bring down the season's curtain at the national stadium on May 26.

Back at Ibrox on a memorable spring afternoon, Larsson and his colleagues went into the encounter knowing they had not won at this ground in seven years, but it was time to set the record straight. Rangers, led by their somewhat arrogant Dutch manager, had hardly been

FLOATING ON AIR...Martin O'Neill has that uplifting feeling as he celebrates another Celtic goal in their 6-2 thrashing of Rangers in his Old Firm debut.

Scottish Premier League Table

P	Team	Pld	W	D	L	GF	GA	GD	Pts
1	**Celtic**	**38**	**31**	**4**	**3**	**90**	**29**	**+61**	**97**
2	Rangers	38	26	4	8	76	36	+40	82
3	Hibernian	38	18	12	8	57	35	+22	66
4	Kilmarnock	38	15	9	14	44	53	–9	54
5	Hearts	38	14	10	14	56	50	+6	52
6	Dundee	38	13	8	17	51	49	+2	47
7	Aberdeen	38	11	12	15	45	52	–7	45
8	Motherwell	38	12	7	19	42	56	–14	43
9	Dunfermline Athletic	38	11	9	18	34	54	–20	42
10	St Johnstone	38	9	13	16	40	56	–16	40
11	Dundee United	38	9	8	21	38	63	–25	35
12	St Mirren	38	8	6	24	32	72	–40	30

League Cup Final

March 18, 2001: **CELTIC 3** Larsson (3)
KILMARNOCK 0

Gould; Mjallby, Vega, Valgaeren; Healy, Lambert, Lennon, Moravcik (sub: Smith), Petta (sub: Crainey; sub: Boyd); Larsson and Sutton.

Scottish Cup Final

May 26, 2001: **CELTIC 3** McNamara, Larsson (2,1 pen)
HIBS 0

Douglas; Mjallby, Vega, Valgaeren; Agathe, Lambert (sub: Boyd), Lennon, Moravcik (sub: McNamara), Thompson (sub: Johnson); Larsson, Sutton.

SWEDE DREAMS...Henrik Larsson takes the plaudits of his team-mates again after his stunning League Cup Final hat-trick against Kilmarnock. Lubomir Moravcik, Stephen Crainey, Ramon Vega and Joos Valgaeren share the joy.

gracious in acknowledging the superiority of Celtic in relieving them of their championship. On the day of the game, Advocaat declared vaingloriously that Rangers, at their strongest, were "more than a match for Celtic".

There can be no doubt the home side were more than a little eager to take the gloss off O'Neill's achievement. And this was most certainly a line-up pieced together by the Irishman with six of the starters in Govan being brought to the club by the new manager since the summer; Rab Douglas, Ramon Vega, Joos Valagaeren, Didier Agathe, Neil Lennon and Alan Thompson. Chris Sutton would surely have represented a seventh, but injury ruled him out.

It was deadlocked at 0-0 until the sixty-first minute when Lubomir Moravcik accepted a cute pass from Larsson, burst into the box and almost casually lifted the ball away from Klos. The Slovakian's second thirteen minutes later was even more accomplished. A low trajectory kick-out from Douglas was headed on by seventeen-year-old Shaun Maloney, making a surprise debut appearance as a second-half substitute for Tommy Johnson.

Moravcik, roaming on the left, checked inside the unfortunate Ricksen and thumped the ball in at the near post from eight yards. And, thus, the little conjuror had bagged two goals against the Ibrox side, just as he did in his first Old Firm game in the autumn of 1998. Larsson completed the rout three minutes from the end with his delicious finish for his fiftieth goal of a mesmerising personal campaign.

The victory equalled most Celtic wins over their bitterest rivals since 1983.

Martin O'Neill had offered Moravcik a one-year extension in an attempt to persuade him to remain and enjoy the forthcoming party nights in Paradise. He hoped the Slovakian, who would be thirty-six years old by the time the new season came around, might agree life in the hoops would be too enjoyable for him to turn his back on it.

O'Neill, playing the crafty Irishman, also got in touch with Jozef Venglos to have a word with his protégé. The good doctor was happy to do so. He asked: "Lubo, do you feel you can still make a contribution at this level? If you believe you can, you must stay. Are you happy? If you are, you must stay. Playing is the best part of football. Carry on while you can because these days will never be repeated."

Moravcik telephoned O'Neill early in the pre-season to say he would be delighted to remain a Celtic player for another twelve months.

It had been an enthralling first season at Parkhead for O'Neill as he watched his team win the Scottish Cup and the League Cup with 3-0 victories over Hibs and Kilmarnock. On March 18, Larsson thumped in a brilliant hat-trick as ten-man Celtic, with Chris Sutton red-carded, thrashed their Ayrshire opponents.

And the unstoppable Swede took centre stage in the Scottish Cup showdown on a gloriously sunny afternoon at the national stadium on May 26. Substitute Jackie McNamara, on for the injured Moravcik, got the ball rolling with the opener before Larsson took over to claim two more in the second-half.

Celtic had not only won the treble, they had done it with style and a flourish reminiscent of Jock Stein's all-conquering Lisbon Lions of another era. ■

READY FOR TAKE-OFF...Alan Thompson prepares for celebrations after scoring the crucial winner against Rangers.

HANDS UP...if you've scored fifty goals! Henrik Larsson celebrates after hitting the half-century against Rangers.

NEIL LENNON... midfield enforcer.

DIDIER AGATHE... Bhoy Racer.

Strip, Strip Hooray

SOME things never change with Celtic ruling the roost in Scottish football for the past three seasons.

However, the Hoops had occasion to alter their playing gear six times as they went about conquering all before them.

As is the custom these days, the Parkhead side had two change strips for each campaign and wing wonder James Forrest, who won several Player of the Year honours this time around, was the perfect role model.

One thing is certain – if you are looking for a consistent performer in this Celtic line-up you can put your shirt on the Scotland international forward. ■

SEASONS 2016 – 2019

Bye Bye, Brendan

BRENDAN RODGERS stunned the Celtic fans with his swift exit on the morning of February 26, 2019 as he quit the champions and agreed a three-year deal with Leicester City.

But, as the day's astonishing turn of events settled, he took the opportunity to thank the Hoops followers for their support during his 33-month stint at Parkhead.

Rodgers, who won back-to-back clean sweeps and was on the brink of a historic treble treble, said it had been "a real honour" to work for the club he had supported growing up in Northern Ireland.

In a statement on the Celtic website, Rodgers said: "It has been a real honour to serve the club and its supporters across the past three seasons.

"I have been a Celtic supporter all my life and the reason I came to Glasgow was to work for the club I had such love and affection for.

"From the moment I walked into Celtic Park, I have been living my dream and, together with the players, staff and supporters, we have been on an amazing journey, which I will never forget.

"To be welcomed in the way I was on my first day at Celtic Park is something I will always treasure. From that day I have given my all to the role of Celtic manager. I would like to sincerely thank the Board at Celtic for giving me the opportunity to manage Celtic in the first place and for the support they have given me throughout my time as manager.

"It has been an absolute pleasure to work with Peter, Ian, Dermot and the rest of the Celtic Board and together we have done everything we could to bring success to our supporters.

"I want to make a special mention to the Celtic players. They were an absolute pleasure to work with and I want to thank them all for the commitment and positivity they gave to my coaching philosophy each and every day.

"Every one of them will be a friend for life.

"Celtic is in great hands for the future and I am sure the club is in a wonderful position to continue to dominate Scottish football and do well in Europe, I know that will be the aim of everyone at the club.

"Celtic will always be my club and I wish everyone connected to Celtic – the Board of Directors, the staff and, of course, the Celtic supporters – every success in the future."

THE EUROPEAN LAST STAND...Brendan Rodgers watches on as Celtic lose to Valencia at Parkhead on February 14.

START OF THE END...Rodgers with the Valencia manager.

HAPPIER DAYS...Rodgers with the Celtic players after his debut title success.

...and Hello Lenny!

WELCOME BACK...Neil Lennon before, during and after his winning return against Hearts at Tynecastle on February 27.

NEIL LENNON rubberstamped his extraordinary return to Celtic at Hampden in the immediate aftermath of the emarkable and dramatic 2-1 Scottish Cup Final ictory on May 25.

The manager, who had been working in an interim apacity since replacing Brendan Rodgers in February, as offered the post on a full-time basis only minutes ollowing the triumph over Hearts that brought the nprecedented treble treble.

Lennon revealed a "five-minute conversation" with hief executive Peter Lawwell, largest shareholder Dermot esmond and director Tom Allison while he was "dripping champagne" provided him with a potentially "life-hanging moment".

After playing what he said was "just a small part" in n "historic" achievement that came with a "weight of xpectation", he can now look forward to building on his ear-five years in charge across two trophy-laden spells.

"I've had highs and lows, which is good, more xperienced, a bit more nous about the game and maybe ot as aggressive as I once was, but I'm still very competitive nd still want to win," said the overjoyed Irishman.

"I've had to learn on the job here about myself, it was different piece of management this time because it didn't el like it was mine and I had to coax it and cajole and get over the line as best as I could."

The 47-year-old former club captain took over from odgers after his sudden departure for Leicester City and d the Hoops to their eighth successive title as well as the mazing ninth consecutive piece of domestic silverware in rollercoaster season that has been littered with unexpected vists and turns.

Discussing winning the league and Cup double in three dramatic months, Lennon smiled: "If anyone had said that I'd have said Hibs are in for a right good time this year!

"That's just the way football is. I work hard. Despite what people think, I'm very professional and I take the job very seriously. I love it, but I'm very, very professional and sometimes you get rewarded for that."

Lawwell maintained the job offer would have been made irrespective of the Hampden outcome and Lennon had no problem about only discovering about being given the "privilege" to manage Celtic again, as he did from 2010 to 2014, until after the Cup Final.

He added: "It keeps you on your toes. It was challenging, but I have complete trust in these guys. I had four great years working under the board, four great years, great times and when the time came we sat down and shook hands and left on very cordial terms.

"I have always kept in touch with Peter and he has kept an eye on my career and been a great support to me.

"It is a privilege. It was a privilege the first time. That was nine years ago, I was younger and a bit more robust. Now I have come full circle. I left the club on good terms and I always wanted to come back and manage again.

"It has been hard work, I had a difficult time at Bolton for reasons not within football and then I had a great couple of years at Hibs. I owe them a debt of gratitude for giving me the platform to get back into this position again.

"I never second guessed anything. These guys are class people. I trust them and trust their word and I expected nothing else.

"Obviously, we have had to deal with a lot of speculation and a lot of false news, but they kept me abreast of everything and they were upfront and honest.

"If anyone has ever dealt with Dermot Desmond they will know you get what you see." ■

The Musonda Mystery

CHARLY MUSONDA arrived at Celtic in the second half of season 2017/18 in a blaze of publicity.

The on-loan Chelsea wonderkid made only eight appearances for the Hoops and his temporary transfer was cut short after only four months of an initial one-and-a-half year deal.

Musonda, who was tipped as a future Belgian international superstar, joined the Parkhead side with Brendan Rodgers making the bold claim he had to fight off competition from TWENTY-THREE clubs throughout Europe who were keen on the young forward.

The 22-year-old maverick was expected to take Scottish football by storm, but he disappeared from view after his rare appearances which didn't quite enthuse the Celtic followers – or the manager.

His failure became a genuine mystery with so many experts convinced the champions had done great business with the Stamford Bridge outfit. ■

Mighty Moussa

Celts quids in with Dembele

THERE is always the element of risk in any transfer, but Moussa Dembele must surely rank as one of the best pieces of business done by Celtic.

NET PROFIT...Moussa Dembele scores another goal against Rangers.

The French powerhouse arrived on a cut-price £500,000 deal from Fulham in June 2016 and the champions picked up £19.8million when he was sold to Lyon just over two years later.

Dembele was Brendan Rodgers' first buy for the club only a month after he took over as manager from Norwegian Ronny Deila.

It didn't take long for the energetic striker to become a massive favourite with the Celtic fans, especially with a hat-trick in his derby debut against Rangers, a 5-1 rout in September at Parkhead.

His legendary countryman Zidine Zidane was moved to say: "I do like to watch the young French players and Dembele is a player I am excited about. Now he has to prove himself in Europe – he needs to show what he's capable of."

Dembele certainly lived up to the billing and answered the expectations of his nation's former World Cup-winning captain.

He scored fifty-one goals in ninety-four competitive games and played his part in Celtic's domestic success before quitting to return to France.

All things considered, it was good business by the champions. ■

TREBLE TALK

ODSONNE EDOUARD, the club's most expensive buy at £10million from Paris Saint-Germain last summer, started and finished the scoring for Celtic in season 2018/19.

The elegant French striker claimed the opening goal in the 3-0 Champions League qualifier win over Alashkert in Armenia on July 10, 2018.

And Edouard had the Final say in the Scottish Cup showpiece showdown with Hearts when he netted the second and winning goal in the eighty-second minute.

He claimed twenty-three strikes in a prolific campaign as he led from the front for most of the term after the £19.8million exit from his compatriot Moussa Dembele on the last day of the August transfer deadline and the absence of Leigh Griffiths in 2019 due to personal issues.

SCOTT BAIN took over from Scotland international Craig Gordon for the first game in 2019 – the 2-0 Scottish Cup victory over Airdrie – and remained in place for the remainder of the campaign.

The former Dundee shotstopper made twenty-five consecutive appearances after the turn of the year and also played against Aberdeen in the League Cup Final at Hampden on December 2 where he had a shut-out as the Hoops lifted the silverware with a first-half strike from Ryan Christie.

Not content with filling Gordon's place at Celtic, Bain also took his No.1 shirt for his nation and made his competitive debut in the Euro 2020 Championship qualifier against Kazakhstan. The Hoops star was blameless as the Scots crashed 3-0, a defeat that went a long way to Alex McLeish losing his managerial post.

THE scoring feat of the season belonged to James Forrest who ran amok against St Johnstone at McDiarmid Park in October.

The on-fire winger netted a remarkable FOUR in the first-half of a 6-0 rout of the Perth side.

Proving he was a man for the big occasion, Forrest scored crucial opening goals in the Scottish Cup quarter-final against Hibs at Easter Road and against Aberdeen in the semi-final. Unfortunately, he drew a blank in the silverware shoot-out.

CELTIC brought in a record three loan signings in January as Brendan Rodgers strengthened his squad.

Scotland international forward Oliver Burke arrived from West Brom, German right-back Jeremy Toljan agreed a temporary transfer from Bundesliga outfit Borussia Dortmund and Timothy Weah came in from French giants Paris Saint-Germain.

Filip Benkovic had already arrived on loan from Leicester City in the summer. The Croatian Under-21 international central defender had cost the Midlands outfit £17million when he joined from Dinamo Zagreb in June.

MIKAEL LUSTIG doesn't score many goals, but the Swedish international defender's timing cannot be faulted.

He dived full-length to head a Callum McGregor left-wing cross past Aberdeen keeper Joe Lewis to put the Hoops on their way to title No.8 on May 4. His close-range effort opened the scoring on an afternoon where Jozo Simunovic nodded in the second to match his winner against Kilmarnock the previous month. Odsonne Edouard claimed the third.

Lustig's only other goal came in the 5-1 triumph over Killie at Parkhead in December. ■